Umpiring Baseball

Jay Baum

Produced by Book Developers, Inc.
of Chicago, Illinois,
for Contemporary Books, Inc.

Contemporary Books, Inc.
Chicago

Library of Congress Cataloging in Publication Data

Baum, Jay.
    Umpiring baseball.

    Includes index.
    1. Baseball—Umpiring.   I. Title.
GV876.B38   1978   796.357'077   78-24181
ISBN 0-8092-7476-0

Copyright © 1979 by Book Developers, Inc.
All rights reserved
Published by Contemporary Books, Inc.
180 North Michigan Avenue, Chicago, Illinois 60601
Manufactured in the United States of America
Library of Congress Catalog Card Number: 78-24181
International Standard Book Number: 0-8092-7476-0

Published simultaneously in Canada by
Beaverbooks
953 Dillingham Road
Pickering, Ontario L1W 1Z7
Canada

GENERAL TIPS FOR UMPIRES

, an umpire, you must be so familiar with
e rules that you are able to make accurate
lls quickly during the play of the game.
lf-improvement is achieved mainly
rough experience, but you may contribute
your success by studying the rules and
plying them in case situations. A good um-
re is determined to do a commendable job.
When calling a game, you should strive to
the following:

1. Cooperate with all other umpires.
aintain a professional relationship and
ork as a team.

2. Change a call if your first ruling was
correct. An umpire who recognizes his own
istakes gains respect.

3. Use good judgement. You must be deci-
ve and accurate, as many calls require split-
econd decisions.

4. Be firm and stand behind your correct
alls. You must have the courage to make a
orrect call on a close play that may deter-
ine the outcome of the game.

5. Have confidence in yourself.

6. Present a good appearance. Players
nd coaches will respect you more.

7. Retain your poise. Think before acting
nd remain unshaken in controversial situa-
ions.

8. Always hustle to position yourself so
hat you are able to make accurate calls.

9. Be dependable, reliable, and prompt.

10. Be careful when forming friendly rela-
ionships with coaches and players; it could
ause you unnecessary problems.

Contents

Acknowledgment

Introdu

Special thanks are offered to the National Federation of State High School Associations for permission to reprint their rules at the beginning of each chapter of this book.*

The interpretations and commentary on the rules are entirely those of the author and do not represent the position of the Federation.

As popular as warm weather, peanu Cracker Jack, baseball has been a summer American pastime for more hundred years. Abner Doubleday, ac to popular legend, staged the first baseball game in Cooperstown, New Y 1839 and, by 1845, Andrew J. Car drew up the first official rules—m which are still used today.

To the uninitiated, baseball seems simple game. Some have gone so erroneously, of course—to call it borin ers, umpires, and fans know better. B is a complicated game that can be fairly only by following a well-defin lengthy set of rules.

This book is written for the amate pire who calls the plays on Little diamonds, high school ballparks, sa and park district fields. Each chapter prets a single rule in clear language, fo by a problem situation and a rulin rules quoted are those of the National ation of High School Associations.

*1977-78 National Federation edition, Baseball Rules, Copyright, 1977, by the National Federation of State High School Associations.

EQUIPMENT

An umpire must provide all of his own standard equipment. As a home plate umpire, you will need a chest protector, protective mask, ball sack, shin guards, protective cup, ball-and-strike indicator, and a small whisk broom. A base umpire must have a ball-and-strike indicator and an optional ball sack.

Traditionally, umpires dress in dark slacks and dark shirt, both preferably blue. Some umpires, however, wear a light blue or white shirt with a tie. Either uniform is acceptable. Both should include a regulation cap and a pair of dark shoes. It may seem unnecessary to emphasize, but appearance and bearing do influence how you are viewed by players and coaches.

1

Umpiring

RULE 10

Section 1.—General

ART. 1 . . . GAME OFFICIALS are: umpire in chief and one, two or three field umpires. Any umpire has the authority to order a player, coach, or team attendant to do or refrain from doing anything which affects the administering of these rules, and to enforce prescribed penalties.

ART. 2 . . . If there is only ONE UMPIRE, he has complete jurisdiction in administering the rules and he may take any position he desires (usually behind the catcher, but sometimes behind the pitcher if there are runners).

ART. 3 . . . ANY UMPIRE'S DECISION which involves judgment, such as whether a hit is fair or foul, whether a pitch is a strike or ball, or whether a runner is safe or out, is final. But if there is a reasonable doubt about some decision being in conflict with the rules, the coach or captain may ask that correct ruling be made. The umpire making the decision may ask another umpire for information before making a final decision. No umpire shall criticize or interfere with another umpire's decision unless asked by the one making it.

NOTE: The umpire in chief sometimes asks for aid from the base umpire at third when there is a question as to whether a batter's "half swing" is such as to be called a strike. As an aid in deciding, the umpire may note whether the swing carried the bat halfway across the plate, but final decision is based on whether the batter actually struck at the ball.

ART. 4 . . . NO UMPIRE may be replaced during a game unless he becomes ill or is injured. His right to disqualify players or to remove nonplayers for objecting to decisions or for unsportsmanlike conduct is absolute.

Section 2.—Umpire in Chief

ART. 1 . . . If there are two (or more) umpires, the UMPIRE IN CHIEF shall stand behind the catcher. He shall call and count balls and strikes, signal fair hits, and call out "foul ball" while signaling each foul hit and make all decisions on the batter. He shall make all decisions except those commonly reserved for the field umpire.

ART. 2 . . . THE UMPIRE IN CHIEF has sole authority to forfeit a game, and he has jurisdiction over any rules matters not mentioned in Art. 1, and not assigned to the field umpire in Section 3.

His duties include those listed in Art. 7 and also the following:

a. **Inspect equipment**, condition of field, receive batting order of both teams, announce special ground rules and formulate such if the two teams cannot agree, designate the official scorer and see that each player takes his glove and ·other loose equipment to the bench at the end of his term in the field.

b. **Call "Play ball"** and give beckoning hand signal to start the game or to resume play; and call "Time" whenever ball becomes dead.

c. **Disqualify** player or clear the bench or send coach from the field if it becomes necessary.

d. **Announce** each batter and each substitution.

e. **Call game** if conditions become unfit for play.

f. **Penalize** for rule infractions (such as balk, interference, delay, unwarranted disputing of decision, or unsportsmanlike conduct).

g. **Make final decision** on points not covered by the rules.

h. **Forfeit** the game for prescribed infractions by spectators, players or attendants.

i. **When game is played** under the auspices of an organization which permits protests to be filed, he shall report the protest to the organization along with all related conditions at the time of the protested play, provided the protest is entered by the offended team at the time of the play and before the next pitch after such play.

j. **Keep a record of defensive team**

charged conferences for each team and notify the respective coach each time a conference is charged to his team.

Section 3.—Field Umpire

ART. 1 . . . A FIELD UMPIRE shall aid the umpire in chief in administering the rules. He shall make all decisions on the bases except those reserved for the umpire in chief. He shall have concurrent jurisdiction with umpire in chief in calling time, balks, defacement or discoloration of ball by the pitcher, use of illegal pitch, when a fly ball is caught, or in disqualifying any player for flagrant, unsportsmanlike conduct or infraction as prescribed by the rules.

ART. 2 . . . When there is only ONE FIELD UMPIRE, he shall make all decisions at first and second and such decisions at third as cannot be more conveniently made by the umpire in chief.

ART. 3 . . . IF ADDITIONAL field umpires are used, they are referred to as base umpires and their normal positions are behind third and second bases. They have concurrent jurisdiction with the first field umpire.

INTERPRETATION

General

The officials for the game include an umpire in chief, and either one, two, or three field umpires. There must be at least one umpire in order for an official game to be played. If there is only one umpire judging the game, he has, of course, complete jurisdiction in administering the rules. All umpires have the right to enforce penalties, as well as to order all persons to follow the rules of the game. They have absolute authority to remove anyone from a game for displaying unsportsmanlike conduct. When an umpire makes a judgment call, that decision is considered final.

If questions arise concerning an alternate ruling, time may be called to discuss the rule. Umpires may confer with each other before making a final decision. Sometimes the home plate umpire may request judgment from a field umpire stationed behind first or third base, for example to determine whether a batter swung far enough around for a pitch to be called a strike.

Protests—when allowed—may only question rule interpretations, not judgment calls. An umpire may be replaced during a game only if he becomes injured or ill.

Umpire in Chief

The umpire in chief stands behind the catcher and is responsible for calling balls and strikes on the batter. He also determines the difference between fair hits and foul balls. As umpire in chief, you must signal your calls in either case, and when a ball is foul, you must shout "foul ball" in addition to using the hand signal.

The umpire in chief is the only umpire with authority to forfeit a game. He has complete jurisdiction on all calls and rules that are not specifically assigned to the field umpire. In addition to the above responsibilities, as umpire in chief you have the following duties:

1. Inspect the players' equipment and the playing field.

2. Receive the batting orders and announce the ground rules.

3. Designate an official scorer.

4. Make sure each player takes his glove and all other loose equipment to the bench at the end of every half-inning.

5. Call out "play ball" and "time" when appropriate.

6. Announce each batter and all substitutes.

7. Call the game, providing the conditions are unfit for play.

8. Assess penalties for rule infractions.

9. Make the final decisions on any points which are not covered by the rules.

10. Declare forfeits.

11. File a report to the league directors when a game is protested.

12. Record defensive and offensive charged conferences.

Field Umpire

The field (or base) umpires usually make all the calls on the bases, although sometimes the home plate umpire may make a call on the bases. As a field umpire you may do any of the following:

1. Call time.

2. Call balks, illegal pitches, or defacement of the ball by the pitcher.

3. Call an out.

4. Remove any player or coach from the game.

When only one base umpire assists the umpire in chief, he makes all the calls at first and second base, and also any calls at third base which cannot be handled by the home plate umpire. These situations are covered in more depth in the section on mechanics.

When additional umpires are used, they are stationed behind second and third base and make appropriate calls at their respective bases.

MECHANICS OF COVERAGE
Umpire in Chief Without Field Umpires

The umpire in chief stands behind the catcher and makes all the calls and decisions throughout the game. (If there is no umpire equipment, the umpire should position himself behind the pitcher. This type of positioning should be avoided if possible.)

The key to umpiring without the assistance of a field umpire is to station yourself at an angle so that all plays are in view. The lone umpire must get "out" on the bases to make many action calls, but if a play occurs at the plate, he must be in position to make that call also. In order to accomplish this, you have to hustle. Consider a typical play: The batter hits a ground ball to the shortstop who will try throwing the batter-runner out at first base. In order to make an accurate call, you should run at least halfway to first base.

There's a simple procedure for making a call at first base: watch the base and listen for the sound of the ball hitting the first baseman's mitt. If the runner's foot has not touched the base, and you hear a loud "thud" from the mitt, you know the runner is out. If the runner's foot is on the base or past it when you hear the "thud" of the mitt, you know the runner is safe.

If you are umpiring without assistance, station yourself halfway between the two bases with the action. If there is a potential play at home plate, position yourself between first base and home plate so you can make the call at either first or home. A good umpire anticipates the location of a potential play.

Calling balls and strikes on the batter is probably the most important duty of the home plate umpire. Stand close to the catcher in order to get the best view of the ball coming toward the plate. If you stand too far from the plate, it is difficult to call the low pitch. It is important, however, not to touch or otherwise interfere with the catcher.

If the count is a full (three balls and two strikes) hold both hands up in a fist rather than using any fingers.

To indicate the number of balls and strikes, raise your fingers and display your hands, so that the number is clearly seen even from the outfield. Display the number of strikes on the fingers of your right hand and the number of balls on your left hand. If the count is full (three balls and two strikes), put both hands up in a fist rather than using any fingers.

Umpire in Chief and One Field Umpire

The field umpire's position depends on whether or not runners are on base. If there are no runners on base, the field umpire stations himself about ten feet behind first base,

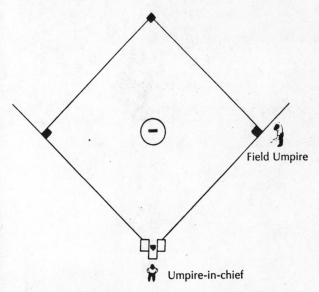

With no runners on base, the field umpire stands about ten feet behind first base. When a ball is batted, he makes all calls except at home plate.

slightly in foul territory. In this situation the field umpire is in charge of making all base calls except those at home plate.

With a runner on first, or runners on both first and second, the field umpire stations himself approximately halfway between the pitcher and second base, slightly toward the first-base side. In this position, the umpire can comfortably make all calls at first and second base. The home plate umpire is then responsible for home plate and, if possible, third base. The field umpire should cover calls at third base whenever the home plate umpire cannot get there. Before the game,

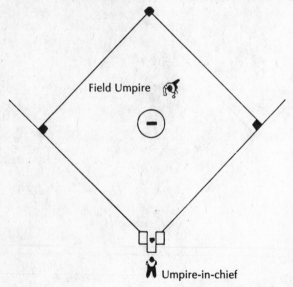

Field Umpire

Umpire-in-chief

With a runner on first, or runners on both first and second, the field umpire should stand approximately halfway between the pitcher and second base.

the umpire in chief should tell the field umpire in which situations he is most likely to need help covering third base.

When runners are on second and third, the field umpire should position himself halfway between the pitcher and second base, slightly toward the third base side. This enables the umpire to make a call at second or third and allows him to get into position for making accurate calls at first.

As a field umpire you must not block the shortstop's or second baseman's view. The umpire's positioning should be flexible.

If a runner is on third base, the field um-

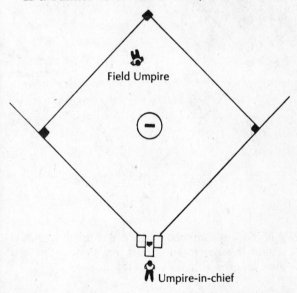

When runners are on second and third, the field umpire positions himself halfway between the pitcher and second base, slightly toward the left field side.

pire stations himself behind first base (the same positioning he assumes if there are no runners), because the most likely play will occur at first base.

Umpire in Chief and Two Field Umpires

With no runners on base the umpires station themselves about ten feet behind first and third bases, slightly into foul territory. The

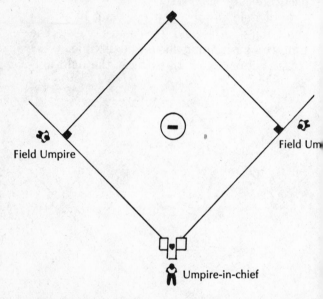

Field Umpire

Field Um

Umpire-in-chief

Without any runners on base the umpires should station themselves about ten feet behind first and third bases, slightly into foul territory.

umpire at third base makes all calls at second, as well as those occurring at third.

With any runners on base, the umpires are positioned as in Figure 1-6.

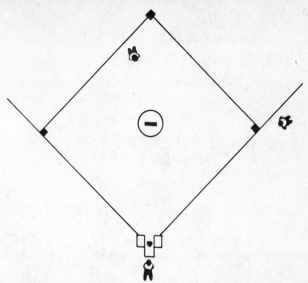

With any runner on base, the umpires should be
positioned as above.

Each umpire is stationed behind one of the bases
and officiates at that base.

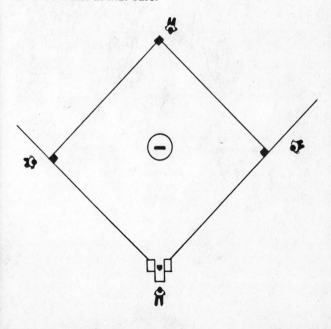

Umpire in Chief and Three Field Umpires

Each umpire positions himself behind one of the bases and is responsible for all decisions at that base.

NATIONAL FEDERATION BASEBALL UMPIRE'S SIGNALS

Do not pitch
and time-out

Play ball

Ball dead immediately
as for batter being hit
by pitch or batted ball
touched by spectator

Delayed dead ball
as for balk or
catcher interference

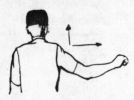

Strike

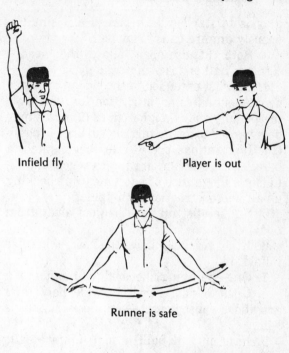

Infield fly

Player is out

Runner is safe

Fair or foul ball

Umpire's Signals:

1. Right arm straight out front with palm outward and fingers up—signifies don't pitch and ball is dead.

2. Beckoning motion with right hand at head level while facing pitcher—signifies

play is to start or be resumed and simultaneously umpire calls "Play ball."

3. Both hands open above the head—signifies ball is dead immediately.

4. Left fist extended to the side at shoulder height—signifies an infraction for which: (1) the penalty may be ignored; or (2) bases may be awarded after no further advance is possible. Illustrations are: (1) an illegal pitch, a balk, catcher or umpire interference; and (2) fielder's illegal use of equipment in checking a ball and obstruction by a fielder.

5. Strike—fist up and then out away from body.

6. Right fist held above the head—signifies infield fly.

7. Out—pumping clenched fist motion.

8. Open hands moved in wide horizontal arc above waist height—signifies a runner is safe.

9. Fair or foul ball; if foul, umpire calls "Foul ball."

2

Players' and Field Equipment

RULE 1

Section 1.—Positions and Equipment of Players

ART. 1 . . . IN HIGH SCHOOL BASEBALL, EACH TEAM is permitted seven turns at bat during which it attempts to score runs by having its batters become baserunners who advance to and touch first base, second base, third base, and home plate (base). The team in the field attempts to end each turn at bat of the opponent by causing three of its batters or baserunners to be out. Each of the two teams consists of at least nine players throughout the game, one of whom must be designated captain. He and the coach represent the team in communications with umpires. The captains' duties can include: providing the umpire in chief with the name, shirt number, position, and batting order of each starting player; and informing all players as to special ground rules as announced by the umpire in chief.

ART. 2 . . . A PLAYER IS DESIGNATED in the score book by name, shirt number, and by fielding position. A customary arrangement of the fielders is shown by the diagram.

ART. 3 . . . AT THE TIME OF THE PITCH, all fielders shall be on fair ground except the catcher who shall be in the catcher's box.

ART. 4 . . . A PLAYER may change to a different fielding position at any time except that a pitcher, after being listed as such on the official lineup card handed in to the umpire, cannot change until conditions in 3-1-1 and 2 are met. Changes must be reported to the umpire for announcement.

PLAY—Fielder F^6 desires to exchange positions with pitcher F^1 when batter B^1 has a strike or ball. RULING: Legal, provided retiring pitcher has pitched to at least one batter until he has completed his time at bat or there has been a third out.

ART. 5 . . . UNIFORMS of all team members should be of the same color and style. Caps and shoes are required equipment (no track spikes allowed). Shoe sole or heel projections other than the standard shoe plate are prohibited. When a player is required to wear a head protector, it replaces the cap as mandatory equipment. For individual players, uniform sleeves lengths may vary; however, sleeves of each individual player shall be approximately the same length and shall not be ragged, frayed nor slit. If the pitcher's undershirt sleeves are exposed they shall not be white or gray in color. A uniform shall not have any dangerous or reflective buttons or ornaments. Each player shall be numbered on the back of his shirt with a plain number of solid color contrasting with color of shirt. The number shall be at least eight inches high and no players on the same team shall wear identical numbers.

It is mandatory for each batter, runner, and the catcher to wear a head protector. The head protector shall be a type which has safety features equal to or greater than those provided by the full plastic cap with padding on the inside. The head protector worn by each batter and each runner shall have extended ear flaps which cover both ears and temples. The liner type head protector does not meet these rules specifications. When an umpire witnesses a runner (including the batter-runner) deliberately remove his head protector during playing action, the violator shall be declared out immediately, unless the ball becomes dead without being touched by a fielder or unless the head protector is removed after the ball becomes dead following its touching by a fielder. The catcher shall wear in addition to his head protector a mask, body protector, and a protective cup. Any player warming up a pitcher at home plate shall wear a mask. It is recommended that any player warming up a pitcher at any other location wear a mask. When an umpire orders a batter or runner to wear a head protector or a catcher to wear a head protector, mask, protective cup and/or body protector, the failure by the player to do so shall cause his dismissal from the game. If the pitcher wears a head protector its entire outer cover shall have a nonglare surface. A pitcher shall not wear any item on his hands, wrists, or arms which may be distracting to the batter.

LOOSE EQUIPMENT (such as gloves) of the team at bat may not be on or near the field.

Section 2—The Field

ART. 1 . . . A DIAMOND (or infield) shall be a ninety-foot square. The outfield is the area between two foul lines formed by extending two sides of the diamond as in the diagram. All lines on the playing field shall be marked with a material which is not injurious to the eyes or skin. Lime or caustic material of any kind is prohibited. Distance from home plate to the nearest obstruction on fair ground should be at least 300 feet down the foul lines and at least 350 feet to centerfield. It is recommended that the line from home base through the pitcher's plate to second base should run east-northeast. The catcher's box, home plate, bases, coaches' boxes, batters' boxes, and three-foot first base lines shall be as in the diagram. The base lines shall be level and the diamond surface gradually sloped up to the pitcher's plate which shall be ten inches above the base line level. On a sodded field, an unsodded area, commonly referred to as the "pitcher's mound," should have a radius of about nine feet with center one and one-half feet in front of the midpoint of the front edge of the pitcher's plate. The infield and outfield, including the boundary marks from home plate to first and third and their extended foul lines are fair ground. All other area is foul ground.

Section 3.—Equipment

ART. 1 . . . FIRST, SECOND, AND THIRD BASE shall be white bags made of canvas, rubber, or synthetic material and must be securely attached to the ground.

Shape: 15 inch square   Thickness:
Filling: Soft material   2 to 5 inches

NOTE: If a base breaks loose from its fastening when a runner slides against it the runner is not out if he should then be tagged.

ART. 2 . . . HOME PLATE (base) shall be a five-sided slab of whitened rubber or other suitable similar material. It shall be a twelve-inch square with two of the corners filled in so that one edge is seventeen inches long, two are eight and one-half inches, and two are twelve inches. It shall be set in the ground so that the two twelve-inch edges coincide with the diamond lines extending from home base to first base and to third base with the seventeen-inch edge facing the pitcher's plate.

ART. 3 . . . THE PITCHER'S PLATE shall be a rectangular slab of whitened rubber or suitable material, twenty-four inches by six inches. It shall be set in the ground as shown in the diagram so that the distance between the nearer edge of the pitcher's plate and the home base intersection of the diamond lines shall be sixty feet six inches.

ART. 4 . . . THE BALL shall be a sphere

formed by yarn wound around a small core of cork, rubber, or similar material and covered with two strips of white horsehide or two strips of white cowhide tightly stitched together. It shall be:

In weight: 5 to 5¼ ounces; in circumference: 9 to 9¼ inches

For interscholastic games, the reaction of the ball shall be similar to that of balls used in professional league play and such as to meet the specifications of the sponsoring organization. The home team shall provide enough balls to permit the game to proceed without unnecessary delay.

ART. 5 . . . THE BAT shall be a smooth cylinder with either a knob or with a handle end tapered to prevent slippage. It is mandatory that the knobs on aluminum or magnesium bats be securely fastened. The aluminum or magnesium bats must have a sound deadening material inside. The bat may be roughened or wound with tape or twine not more than eighteen inches from the handle end of the bat. The bat shall be:

In diameter at thickest part	2 ¾ or less
In length	42″ or less

ART. 6 . . . THE LEATHER GLOVES OR MITTS used by players must conform to the following specifications:

Position	Size around Palm	Webbing from Thumb to Finger
Catcher	No limit	No limit
Pitcher*	14"	No limit
1st Baseman	12" or less long by 8" or less across palm	Leather lacing 4" or less and no other extension or reinforcement
Others	14"	No limit

No limit on weight of glove or mitt for any position.

Only the catcher and the first baseman may wear either a leather glove or mitt. All other fielders may wear only a leather glove.

*Pitcher's glove must be of one color and neither white nor gray.

Section 4—Defective Field and Player Equipment

ART. 1 . . . DEFECTIVE EQUIPMENT must be repaired or replaced immediately.

INTERPRETATION
Positions and Equipment of Players

In high school baseball and other amateur leagues a game lasts seven innings. If the game is tied after the regulation seven innings, extra innings are played to break the tie. An inning consists of two parts, a top half and a bottom half. The visiting team always bats first, in the top half of the inning, and the home team bats last, in the bottom half of the inning.

Each team gets seven chances to bat and seven times in the field. There is one exception, however. If the home team is ahead after six and one-half innings, there is no need for them to bat in the bottom of the seventh. It should be noted that in some Little Leagues the games last only six innings.

The object of the game is to score runs, which can be done only when a team is at bat. The batter must become a baserunner, and touch all bases—first, second, third, and home plate—for a run to count. The half-running is over when the team in the field gets three outs on the team at bat. The two teams then switch positions; the fielding team coming in for a turn at bat, and the hitting team takes the field.

Each team must have nine players on the field at all times. One of the players, usually elected by his teammates or selected by the manager, is designated the captain. He plays an important role. Besides the obvious leadership responsibilities, the captain is the only player, excluding a coach, who is allowed to confer with an umpire about a call or rule interpretation. He must also turn in the starting lineup and inform his teammates of the ground rules discussed before the game with the umpires and opposing team captain and coaches.

In the official scorebook, the players are designated by name, shirt number, and field position. Each position is labeled by a number for consistency in scorekeeping. Figure 2-1 labels the players by position and number.

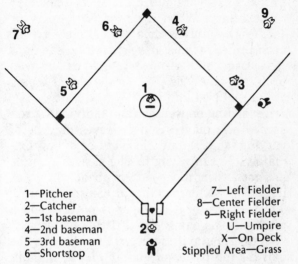

1—Pitcher
2—Catcher
3—1st baseman
4—2nd baseman
5—3rd baseman
6—Shortstop

7—Left Fielder
8—Center Fielder
9—Right Fielder
U—Umpire
X—On Deck
Stippled Area—Grass

Diagram 2-1 labels the players by position and number.

The left fielder, for example, is designated by a 7 and the second baseman by a 4.

All players except the catcher must be in fair territory at the time of a pitch. The catcher crouches behind the plate in the catcher's box.

Players may change fielding positions at any time, provided the change is reported to the umpire in chief. There is one exception to this rule, however, and it involves the pitcher (see Chapter 4—Rule 3).

All team members and coaches must wear uniforms that are similar in color and style. Players must wear caps and athletic shoes. Track spikes are not allowed as they may cause injury. When a player bats, runs, or catches, he must wear a head protector. The head protector must have extending ear flaps that cover both ears and temples. A head protector takes the place of the cap as a part of the required uniform.

Depending on weather and individual preference, the players' shirt sleeves may be of varying lengths, but all should be of approximately the same length. The sleeves must be in good condition—not ripped, torn, or frayed. A tattered uniform can cause problems, especially if a player is batting and a pitch hits his baggy shirt. If this happens, it is up to the umpire to determine whether the ball hit the batter or simply nicked the uniform. A good umpire, however, won't get in this position; he would not let a player bat who is not dressed appropriately. As home plate umpire, you should check each new batter for proper dress and equipment. You need not spend five minutes on inspection; simply glance at the helmet, shoes, bat, and uniform. This is usually enough to notice whether attire is appropriate, and it only takes a few seconds.

Sleeve regulations differ for pitchers. Pitchers may not wear shirts with gray or white sleeves. If this ruling isn't enforced, the batter may not be able to distinguish the ball from the pitcher's shirt sleeve. Also, the pitcher may not wear any items on his hands, wrists, or arms that may distract a batter.

No uniforms may have dangerous items attached, such as reflective buttons or ornaments. Each player must have a number on the back of his shirt; the number must be a solid color that contrasts with the color of the shirt and must be at least eight inches high. No two players on the same team may wear the same number.

In addition to a head protector, a catcher must wear a mask, a chest protector, and protective cup. One rule that is often neglected by umpires requires that "Any player warming up a pitcher at home plate shall wear a mask." Don't overlook it; there is no reason for injury to occur in such a situation.

Loose equipment such as gloves, balls, bats, masks, and head protectors may not be on or near the field as it may interfere with the game.

Situation: Lane Tech is hosting Manley High in a playoff game. In the top of the seventh inning, Lane is ahead 4-2. Manley is threatening with men at second and third base, with two outs. A Manley player lines a hit to right field. The man on third scores easily, and the man on second is heading home when the batter-runner rounds first and deliberately knocks his helmet off so he can run faster. The umpire immediately declares the batter-runner out. Since the runner on second did not touch home before the umpire signaled the batter-runner out, his run did not count. The game ended with Lane Tech winning, 4-3.

Ruling: The umpire made the correct call. According to the rule, the player made the game-ending out immediately when he deliberately knocked off his helmet while the ball was in play.

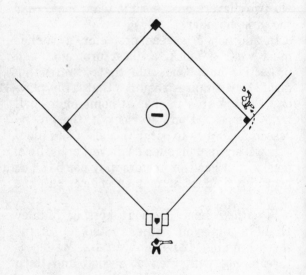

The player made the game-ending out when he knocked off his helmet.

THE FIELD

The baseball infield (diamond) is square, with sides of 90 feet. The outfield is formed by the extension of the two foul lines (at first and third base) beyond the infield. The infield and outfield are fair territory along with the actual foul lines. A ball striking the foul line is ruled fair. The lines are marked with a material that is not injurious to the eyes or skin.

A good way to determine whether a fly ball down the left or right field line is going to be fair or foul is to watch just outside the line. If the ball strikes outside the line, you'll be looking for it and see that it is foul. If it strikes the line, you'll see some of the white material fly up and you will know it's fair. If the ball drops inside the line you'll know it's fair because you *did not* see it drop foul. Sometimes this won't work because the lines may not have been drawn out far enough or they may have been washed out by rain. If this is the case, the umpire has to do his best by drawing a straight line in his mind from home plate to the foul flag. He must make the call as he sees it.

EQUIPMENT

The three bases—first, second, and third—must be white bags which should be securely attached to the ground. They are usually made of canvas, rubber, or a synthetic material. If a runner slides into a base, and in the process unfastens it, the runner is not ruled out even if he has been tagged.

Home plate is a five-sided slab of whitened rubber, that also must be securely fastened to

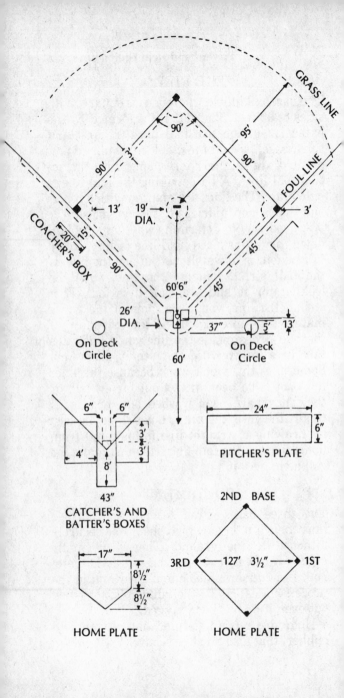

the ground. Two of its sides coincide with the base lines.

The pitcher's plate or pitching rubber is a rectangular slab of whitened rubber, 24 inches by 6 inches. It is usually placed 60 feet, 6 inches from the point of intersection between home plate and the diamond lines. The distance does vary for different leagues and different levels of competition, but it never should exceed 60 feet, 6 inches. In fact, all the field dimensions may be shortened for younger players; this decision is made by league directors.

The ball is made of yarn, cork, rubber, and white cowhide, weighs 5 to $5\frac{1}{4}$ ounces, and is 9 inches in circumference. Usually, the home team supplies the balls and gives them to the umpire in chief. The bats used by both teams must be made in a matter that prevents slippage while swinging the bat. Aluminum or magnesium bats must have a sound-deadening material inside. A player may tape or roughen up a bat up to 18 inches from the handle. All bats must be no more than $2\frac{3}{4}$ inches in diameter and 42 inches or less in length.

The pitcher must use a glove that is one solid color; it cannot be white. Only the catcher may wear a catcher's mitt, and only a first baseman may wear a first baseman's mitt.

It is up to the umpire and coaches to make sure all the equipment is in good working condition. If it is defective, it must be repaired or replaced.

3

Playing Terms and Definitions

RULE 2

Section 1.—Ball, Base on Balls, in Flight, Dead Ball

ART. 1 . . . THE BALL is one of the playing implements. The term is also used to designate a pitch which is not touched by the bat and is not a strike as in 7-2-2. If a batter receives four such balls, he is awarded a BASE ON BALLS (often referred to as a "walk") and must go immediately to first base before timeout is called. AN INTENTIONAL BASE ON BALLS may be given by the defensive team by having its catcher, or coach, request the umpire to award the batter first base. This may be done before pitching to the batter or on any ball and strike count.

ART. 2 . . . A BATTED OR THROWN BALL IS IN FLIGHT until it has touched the ground or some object on fair or foul ground, or it has touched a person other than a fielder while the ball is over foul ground.

ART. 3 ... BALL BECOMES DEAD when acts listed in 5-1 occur.

Section 2.—Batter, Batter's Box, B^1, B^2

ART. 1 ... THE BATTER is the player of the team at bat who is entitled to occupy either of the two batter's boxes as shown on the diagram. THE BATTER'S BOX is the area in which the batter shall stand with both his entire feet when batting. The lines forming the box are a part of it. An ON DECK CIRCLE for each team is a circle 5 feet in diameter located 37 feet at each side of and 13 feet behind home plate.

ART. 2 ... THE PLAYER WHO BATS FIRST in his half of an inning is designated B^1. The third player to bat is B^3. Base runners are designated R^1 for the one farthest in advance, R^2 and R^3.

Section 3.—Catch, Catcher, Catcher's Box

ART. 1 ... A CATCH is the act of a fielder in getting secure possession in his hand or glove of a live ball in flight and firmly holding it, provided he does not use his cap, protector, mask, pocket, or other part of his uniform to trap the ball. It is considered a catch if a fielder catches a fair or foul ball and then steps or falls into a bench, dugout, stand, bleacher, or over any boundary or barrier, such as a fence, rope, chalk line, or a pregame determined imaginary boundary line from the field of play. Falling into does not include merely running against such object. See 2-13-2 for baseman juggling ball and 8-4-1-b for intentionally dropped ball. See 2-8-2-

P.R. (3) and 5-1-1-c for ball striking catcher before touching his glove. It is not a catch when a fielder touches a batted ball in flight which then contacts a member of the offensive team or an umpire and is then caught by a defensive player.

NOTE: When a batted ball or a pitch is involved, the above definition of catch applies. For any other thrown ball, the term is used loosely to also apply to a pickup or to the trapping of a low throw which has touched the ground. A fielder may have the ball in his grasp even though it is touching the ground while in his glove.

ART. 2 ... THE CATCHER is the player to whom the pitcher throws when delivering the ball to the batter. When he is in position to receive a pitch, he must be in the catcher's box as stated in 6-1-1.

Section 4.—Charged Conferences

ART. 1 ... A CHARGED CONFERENCE is one which involves the coach or his representative and a player or players of the team.

Section 5.—Errors, Passed Ball, Interference, Obstruction

ART. 1 ... AN ERROR is a misplay by a fielder as listed in 9-5-5, and which is recorded in the error column of the player's record.

ART. 2 ... A PASSED BALL is a pitch which the catcher fails to stop or control when he should have been able to do so with ordinary effort, and which enables a runner (other than the batter-runner) to advance. If on a third strike, the catcher drops the ball or allows it to go past him when he should have been able to stop it, and if the batter-runner reaches first base, the catcher is charged with an error (not a passed ball).

ART. 3 . . . INTERFERENCE is illegal touching of the ball or hindrance of a fielder by anyone connected with the team at bat. It is UMPIRE INTERFERENCE when he inadvertently moves so as to hinder a catcher's attempt to throw or when a fair ball touches an umpire as in 5-1-1-e. It is DEFENSIVE INTERFERENCE when a catcher or fielder hinders a batter as in 5-1-2-c, 8-1-1-e, 8-3-1-c and 8-3-3. SPECTATOR INTERFERENCE is an action by a spectator which impedes the progress of the game. When interference occurs, the ball becomes dead except as outlined in 5-1-2-b and -c. OBSTRUCTION is illegal hindrance of a runner by a fielder as in 5-1-3 and 8-3-2. When obstruction occurs, the ball does not become dead and the umpire has authority to determine which base or bases shall be awarded the runners.

ART. 4 . . . OTHER MISPLAYS which are not recorded in error column but which are included in game summary include: balk (6-2-4); wild pitch (9-6-1); batter hit by pitched ball (8-1-1-d).

Section 6.—Fielder, Infielder, Outfielder, Battery, F^1, F^2

ART. 1 . . . A FIELDER is any one of the nine players of a team when it is not at bat (defensive team). The players who play left field, right field, and center field are OUT-

FIELDERS. The others are INFIELDERS. The pitcher and catcher are the BATTERY.

ART. 2 . . . IN THE PLAY RULINGS, a fielder is referred to as F^1, F^2, etc. F^1 is the pitcher, F^2 is the catcher, F^3 is 1st baseman, F^4 is 2nd baseman, F^5 is 3rd baseman, F^6 is short stop, F^7 is left fielder, F^8 is center fielder, and F^9 is right fielder.

Section 7.—Game, Called Game, Tie Game, Inning, Half-Inning, Forfeit

ART. 1 . . . A REGULATION INTERSCHO-LASTIC GAME is seven innings (turns at bat) for each team unless shortened as in 4-2-1 and 2 or unless extra innings are necessary to break a tie score.

A CALLED GAME is one which is ended by order of the umpire in accordance with 4-2.

A SUSPENDED GAME is a called game to be completed at a later time.

ART. 2 . . . AN INNING is that portion of the game which includes a term at bat for each team. A HALF-INNING is the interval during which one team is on offense (batting) and the other is on defense (fielding). A half-inning ends when there is a third out or when, in the last inning, the winning run is scored. In either case, if there is delayed discovery of a possible appeal play, the half-inning is considered ended when the in-fielders have moved off the diamond without any attempt to call an umpire's attention to the claimed irregularity.

An EXTRA INNING is one which extends the game in an attempt to break the tie score

(4-2-6). If necessary to end the game when the score is tied, it is a TIE GAME.

ART. 3 . . . A FORFEITED GAME is one awarded to the opponent of the offending team with a score of 7 to 0 as in 4-3-2.

Section 8.—Hit, Fair Hit, Foul, Foul Tip, Bunt, Base Hit, Infield Fly, Ground Hit, Sacrifice, Extra Base Hit

ART. 1 . . . A FAIR HIT (commonly called FAIR BALL) is a batted ball which settles on fair territory between home and third base, or between home and first base, or which is on or over fair ground when bounding to the outfield past first or third base, or first falls on fair ground on or beyond first or third base, or which touches first, second, or third base, or which, while on or over fair territory touches the person of an umpire or player or which while over fair ground passes out of the playing field in flight.

NOTE: A fly hit or line drive which passes over or inside first or third base in flight and curves to foul ground beyond such base is not a fair hit; but a hit which goes over or through the fence is a fair hit if it is over fair ground when it leaves the field.

PLAY (1)—B³ hits line drive or ground hit which: (a) strikes pitcher's plate; or (b) second base. In either case, it rebounds to foul ground between home and third before touching anyone. RULING: (a) Foul. (b) Fair hit.

PLAY (2)—B³ hits. While ball is in flight or is bouncing near to but outside the path from home to first, F³ drops it while having one or both feet on fair ground. RULING: Not a fair hit. Position of ball at time of touching is the determining factor.

PLAY (3)—Batted ball rolls or bounces on foul ground between home and first, or a fly comes down there. In either case, ball then goes into the field between home and first before touching a person or object while on or over foul ground. RULING: Fair ball if it comes to rest on or is touched over fair ground.

PLAY (4)—B² hits fair line drive and while ball is in flight it strikes umpire who is standing: (a) behind third baseman; or (b) behind pitcher, and in each case ball glances high in air after which fielder catches ball. RULING: In (a) ball remains alive and is considered a fair ground ball after it strikes umpire. B² is not out. In (b) ball becomes dead as soon as it strikes the umpire, B² is awarded first and credited with a single.

ART. 2 . . . A FOUL is a batted ball which settles on foul territory between home and first base, or between home and third base; or that bounds past first or third base on or over foul territory; or that first falls on foul territory beyond first or third base; or that, while on or over foul territory, touches the person of an umpire or a player, or any object foreign to the natural ground.

A FOUL TIP is a batted ball which goes directly and speedily from the bat to the catcher's mitt or hand and is legally caught by any fielder.

PLAY (1)—R¹ is advancing to second when B² hits a foul tip. RULING: Legal advance.

Note that to be a foul tip the ball must be caught.

PLAY (2)—Without touching any person, a ground hit rebounds from the pitcher's plate; or a fly hit touches fair ground between home and first or third and bounces to foul ground without having passed first or third. RULING: Foul hit in either case.

PLAY (3)—A pitch touches bat and without touching catcher's hand or mitt strikes his equipment or body, or that of the umpire. It then rebounds into catcher's hands. RULING: Not a foul tip. Such ball becomes dead when it strikes catcher or umpire.

ART. 3 ... A BASE HIT (also called a safe hit or single) is one which enables the batter to advance to first base without being put out and under conditions outlined in 9-3-2.

An EXTRA BASE HIT is one which enables the batter to advance to 1st base and then to one or more succeeding bases as outlined in 9-3-3. A TWO-BASE HIT (double), THREE-BASE HIT (triple) or HOME RUN enables him to reach second, third or home base, respectively.

A FIELDER'S CHOICE is the act of a fielder with a live ball, who elects to throw for an attempted putout or to retire unassisted any runner or batter-runner, thus permitting the advance of another runner(s). Scorers use the term in the following ways: (a) to indicate the advance of the batter-runner who takes one or more bases when the fielder who handles his batted ball plays on a preceding runner; (b) to indicate the advance of a runner (other than by stolen base or error) while a fielder is trying to put out another runner; and (c) to indicate the advance of runner due to the defensive team's refusal to play on him (an undefended steal).

NOTE: Scorer decides whether the batter is credited with a safe hit or an extra base hit in accordance with 9-2-2.

ART. 4 . . . A BUNT is a fair ball in which the batter does not swing to hit the ball but holds the bat in the path of the ball to tap it slowly to the infield.

NOTE: If an attempt to bunt is a foul ball, it is treated the same as any other foul ball except that if the attempt is by a batter who has two strikes, such batter is out as in 7-4-d.

PLAY—With R^1 on third, B^2 has two strikes when he attempts to bunt and it is a foul. Catcher: (a) does not catch the foul; or (b) catches it. RULING: In either case B^2 is out. In (b) ball does not become dead and R^1 must retouch third unless it is a foul tip.

A SACRIFICE is a bunt which enables any runner to advance or a fly ball which enables a runner to score but which, in either case results in the batter-runner being put out before he reaches first base or which would have resulted in his being put out if the hit had been fielded without error; and provided two were not out when the ball was hit. (A sacrifice is not listed as a "time-at-bat.")

ART. 5 . . . An INFIELD FLY is a fair fly (not including a line drive or an attempted bunt) which can be caught by an infielder with ordinary effort; and provided the hit is made before two are out and at a time when first and second bases or all bases are occupied.

When it seems apparent that a batted ball will be an infield fly, the umpire immediately announces it for the benefit of the runners. If the hit should then prove to be foul, the decision is reversed and it is treated the same as any foul. See 7-4-f for batter being out and right of base runner to advance after retouching his base.

PLAY—With R^1 on second, and R^2 on first, B^3 bunts or swings and hits "pop-up" fly which falls between home and third and cannot be caught by any fielder. RULING: Not an infield fly.

ART. 6 . . . A FLY BALL is a batted ball which rises an appreciable height above the ground. A LINE DRIVE is a batted ball which travels parallel or nearly so with the ground through most of its flight. A GROUND BALL is one which is neither a fly nor a line drive.

Section 9.—Oversliding, Overrunning

ART. 1 . . . OVERSLIDING or OVERRUNNING is the act of a runner who, after touching the base to which he is advancing, allows his momentum to carry him past the base so that he loses contact with it.

For right to overrun first base, see 8-2-4. For cases where a runner is not credited with a stolen base or a batter with an extra base hit, see 9-3-3 and 9-4-1. If a force is involved, 2-12-4 states when touching a base ends a force and P.R. (4) under 9-1-1 covers counting of a score when a third out is made after the force has ended.

PLAY (1)—B^1 hits and overruns first base. In coming to a stop he turns toward second but makes no attempt to advance or feint an advance but returns to touch first. RULING: He may return without liability of being put out.

PLAY (2)—B^1 hits to the fence. He advances to first, second, and third but: (a) he overslides third and is tagged out; or (b) he is not put out at third but he fails to touch second and is declared out when the opponent appeals to the umpire. RULING: (a) B^1 is credited with a second-base hit. (b) B^1 is credited with a base hit.

PLAY (3)—R^1 is stealing second when B^2 receives a fourth ball. R^1 overslides second or, after reaching there, he steps off toward third. In either case, he is tagged. RULING: R^1 is out since ball does not become dead on fourth ball.

Section 10.—Pitcher, Pitch, Pivot Foot

ART. 1 . . . THE PITCHER is the player who is designated in the scorebook as being responsible for delivering (pitching) the ball to the batter. A live ball delivered to the batter is a PITCH. The term implies a legally delivered ball unless otherwise stated. When a pitcher commits a balk and completes his delivery to the batter, it is not considered a pitch unless the balk penalty is ignored. TIME OF THE PITCH is when the pitcher has committed himself to delivering the pitch to the batter. For the windup position the "time of the pitch" occurs when the pitcher first starts any movement of his arm or arms prior to delivering the pitch. For the set position the "time of the pitch" occurs the instant the pitcher separates his hands from the ball in front of his body prior to delivering the pitch. A FEINT is a movement which simulates the start of a pitch or a throw to a base and which is used in an attempt to deceive a runner.

ART. 2 . . . The pitcher's PIVOT FOOT is that foot with which the pitcher contacts the pitcher's plate when he throws the ball. For a left-handed thrower, it is the left foot. See 6-1-1.

ART. 3 . . . A BALK is an illegal act committed by a pitcher with a runner, or runners, on base which entitles each runner to advance one base when the penalty is not ignored.

ART. 4 . . . An ILLEGAL PITCH is a pitch which is delivered to the batter when the pitcher does not have his pivot foot in contact with the pitcher's plate, or which is delivered to the batter in violation of the pitching rule (Rule 6), or which is a quick-return pitch. When an illegal pitch occurs with a runner, or runners, on base, it is ruled a balk.

Section 11.—Penalty

A PENALTY is the loss assessed by the umpire against a player (or team) for a rule infraction. Penalties include: disqualifying offending player; declaring a batter or runner out; awarding a base to batter or runner; awarding a ball to batter (for an illegal pitch when there is no runner); charging batter with a strike (for delay); forfeiting a game; or removing nonplayers from the bench or field.

Section 12.—Play Ball, Play Ruling, Double Play, Force Play, Squeeze Play, Appeal Play

ART. 1 . . . "PLAY BALL" is the order given by the umpire when it is time for the game to begin or to be resumed after having been suspended when he called "Time." The term is also used to denote a unit of action which begins when a pitcher has the ball in his possession in pitching position and ends when ball becomes dead or pitcher again holds the ball while in pitching position.

ART. 2 . . . A PLAY RULING is a statement of a play situation and the correct ruling. It is considered an integral part of the rules and applies to analogous situations.

ART. 3 . . . A DOUBLE PLAY is continuous activity which results in 2 put-outs during a play as defined in Art. 1.

ART. 4 . . . A FORCE PLAY is a play in which a runner (or two or three runners) loses his right to the base he occupies and is forced to advance, because the batter becomes a batter-runner. For a given runner a force play ends as soon as he touches the next base or a following runner is put out at a previous base. When a runner advances beyond a base to which he is forced without touching it, he may be put out as provided in Article 6 below and such out is a force-out.

A FORCE-OUT is a put-out during which a runner who is being forced to advance is tagged out, or is put out by a fielder who holds the ball while touching the base toward which the forced runner is advancing. (See Play 5 under 9-1-1 for special case.)

PLAY—With two out, R^1 is on third and R^2 on first when B^5 hits to short center. R^1 goes home. R^2 delays his advance to second but touches second base. He is then put out on an overslide, the out being made after R^1 touches home base. RULING: The run scores. The force ended as soon as R^2 touched second.

ART. 5 . . . A SQUEEZE play is one in which a runner advances toward home base from third, as the ball is being pitched and during which the batter bunts to permit the runner to score.

ART. 6 . . . An APPEAL play is a situation in which the umpire ignores an observed base running infraction listed below unless his attention is called to it by a player of the offended team before the time of the next legal pitch (2-10-1) or illegal pitch (2-10-4), or prior to an awarded intentional base on balls; and before the infielders leave fair territory if a half-inning is ending. These base running infractions include: failure of a runner to touch base which he passes while advancing or returning; and failure of a runner to touch or retouch the base he legally occupied at time of pitch after he batted ball, which if caught, was first touched. An appeal play to be allowed must be made with a live ball. Player of team in the field may either touch base involved while holding the ball, or tag violating runner with ball or his glove with ball in it and then appeal the violation concerned to the umpire.

Section 13.—Put-Out, Tag-Out, Throw-Out, Strike-Out, Throw

ART. 1 . . . A PUT-OUT is the act of a fielder in retiring a batter or runner. For put-outs credited to the catcher and to other fielders see 7-1-Pen. and 9-5-2. An "OUT" is one of the three required retirements of players of the team at bat.

ART. 2 . . . A TAG-OUT is the putting out of a runner (including the batter-runner), who is not touching his base, by touching him with a live ball or with the glove or hand when the live ball is securely held therein by a fielder. The ball is not considered as having been securely held if it is juggled or dropped after the touching unless the runner deliberately knocks the ball from the hand of the fielder. See 8-4-2-c.

NOTE: If the ball is securely held in hand it is customary for umpire to rule that the ball has touched the runner if that hand or glove clearly touches him.

A THROW-OUT is a put-out caused by a throw to first base to retire a batter-runner or to any other base to which a runner is forced or is required to retouch.

ART. 3 . . . A STRIKE-OUT is the result of the pitcher getting a third strike charged to a batter. This usually results in the batter being out, but does not so result if the third strike is not caught and the batter-runner legally reaches first base.

ART. 4 . . . A THROW is the act of voluntarily losing possession through having the ball leave the hand for a purpose other than a pitch. It may result in the ball being bounced, handed, rolled, tossed or thrown. The term is also used as an abbreviation which means the ball after possession has been lost. Illustration: "a throw goes into the stand."

Section 14.—Run, Runner, Batter-Runner

ART. 1 . . . A RUN is the score made by a runner who legally advances to and touches home base as prescribed in 9-1.

ART. 2 . . . A RUNNER is a player of the team at bat who has finished his time at bat and has not yet been put out. The term includes the batter-runner and also any runner who occupies a base.

ART. 3 . . . A BATTER-RUNNER is a player who has finished his time at bat but has not yet been put out or touched first base.

Section 15.—Speed-up Rules

By state association adoption, speed-up rules may be used.

Section 16.—Stolen Base, Double Steal

A STOLEN BASE is an advance of a runner to the next base without the aid of a base hit, a put-out or a fielding (including battery) error and in accordance with conditions in 9-4. A DOUBLE OR TRIPLE STEAL is one which involves two or three runners, respectively.

Section 17.—Strike Zone

The STRIKE ZONE is that space over home base which is between the batter's armpits and the top of his knees when he assumes his natural batting stance. The umpire shall determine the batter's strike zone according to his usual stance when he swings at a pitch. (See 7-2-1 and 2 for determining whether a pitch is a strike or a ball.)

Section 18.—Team and Player Abbreviations

For brevity in the play rulings, the home team is H and the visiting team V. Players of the team at bat are B^1, B^2, etc. Substitutes are S^1, S^2, etc. Runners are R^1, R^2, or R^3, and R^1 is the runner who has advanced farthest. Fielding players are F^1, F^2, etc., in accordance with diagram on page 5.

Section 19.—Time, Time at Bat

ART. 1 . . . "TIME" is the command of the umpire to suspend play. The ball becomes dead when it is given (See 5-2-1 for when "Time" is called.) The term is also used in recording the length of the game.

ART. 2 . . . TIME AT BAT is the period beginning when a batter first enters the batter's box and continuing until he is put out or becomes a runner. EXCEPTION: A batter is not charged in the records with a time at bat when he makes a sacrifice hit, or he is hit by a pitched ball, or he is awarded a base on balls, or he is replaced before being charged with two strikes, or he is replaced after being charged with two strikes and the substitute does not strike out, or when he advances to first base because of interference by a fielder.

Section 20.—Touching Ball, Base, or Runner

TOUCHING is contact with, and there is no distinction between the act of touching and being touched by. For pitched ball touching batter, or batted ball touching batter or any runner, or catcher touching bat, or player touching a base, or ball touching player or nonplayer, the term applies to contact with any part of the person or his clothing if the clothing is reasonably well fitted.

NOTE: See 8-2-3 for failure to touch home plate; 8-2-6 for retouching base; 1-3-1-Note for base coming loose; and 2-9 for oversliding.

Section 21.—Wild Pitch

A WILD PITCH is one which cannot be handled by the catcher with ordinary effort. See 9-6-1.

INTERPRETATION

The terms used in baseball and defined in Rule 2 are interpreted here in alphabetical order.

The *ball* is one of the playing implements. A pitch that is not a strike and that is not touched by the bat is called a *ball*. If a batter is pitched four balls, he is given a *base on balls*, also called a walk. The team in the field can give the batter an intentional walk by asking the umpire to award first base to the batter. This can be done before the pitcher pitches to the batter or on any ball and strike count.

The *batter* is the player on the offensive team who has the right to hit against the pitcher. He stands with both feet in one of the two *batter's boxes*, depending on whether he bats right- or left-handed. Close by, but far enough away from home plate to be out of the way, are two *on deck circles*, one on either side of the plate. The player due to bat next warms up in the on deck circle.

A *catch* occurs when a fielder gains secure possession of a live ball in his hand or glove. For the catch to be legal, the fielder may not use any part of his uniform to trap the ball and must be standing in live territory. Live territory includes both fair and foul territory and is decided before the game during the discussion of the ground rules. The pitcher, when delivering the ball to a batter, throws to the *catcher*. The catcher must be in the *catcher's box* in order to receive the pitch.

A *charged conference* is a time-out called by a coach or team representative to confer with a player.

An *error* is a misplay by a fielder that allows a batter or runner to advance on the bases. A *passed ball* is a misplay on a pitch by the catcher permitting a runner to advance. The catcher also may be charged with an error for certain other misplays.

There are several types of *interference*. For example, interference is called when anyone connected with the team at bat illegally touches the ball or hinders a fielder, when an umpire accidentally hinders a catcher's attempt to throw, and when a fair ball accidentally touches the umpire. Defensive interference—when a catcher or fielder hinders a batter—is more common, as is spectator interference—when a spectator delays the progress of a game. *Obstruction,* which differs from interference, occurs when a fielder illegally hinders a runner in the field.

There are several other misplays which are not considered errors. These are balks, wild pitches, and hit batsmen (covered elsewhere in this chapter).

A *fielder* is one of the nine defensive players on a team when it is not at bat. *Outfielders* play left, center, or right field; the remainder of the players are *infielders.* The pitcher and catcher make up the *battery.*

A *called game* is a game ended by order of the umpire. If the game is to be completed at another time, it is called a *suspended game.* A *forfeited game* is awarded to the team opposing the one that commits a rule infraction.

A *fair hit* or *fair ball* is a batted ball which meets any one of several requirements. It includes a ball that settles anywhere between the foul lines between first and third base, a ground ball that passes first or third in fair territory, a fly ball in the outfield between the foul lines, and a ball that hits a base. A ground ball that passes first or third in fair territory and then rolls foul is a fair ball.

A *foul ball* is a batted ball that settles in foul territory anywhere between home and first or home and third or a fly ball that lands in foul territory past first and third base. A ground ball that passes first or third in fair territory but takes its first bounce after the base in foul territory is considered foul.

A *foul tip* is distinct from a foul ball, and should be distinguished by the umpire. A foul tip occurs when the batter swings at the ball, tips it with his bat, and the ball lands directly in the catcher's mitt. To call a foul tip, listen for the sound of the tip off the bat, and make sure the catcher catches it cleanly.

A *base hit* or *single* is a hit that allows a batter to get to first without being put out. When the batter is able to get to a base past first, the hit is called an *extra-base hit*. If he gets to second it is called a *two-base hit* or *double*, and if he makes it to third it is called a *three-base hit* or *triple*. A *home run* is a hit that allows the batter to round all three bases and make it back to home plate without being put out.

A *fielder's choice* is a play by a fielder that puts out a batter or runner but allows one or more other runners to advance on the bases. For example: there are runners on first and second with one out. A ground ball is hit directly to the shortstop, who fields the ball and quickly throws it to third base to force out the runner coming from second. This enables the runner on first to go to second, and the batter to get to first.

A *bunt* is a strategic offensive play by a batter who taps the ball slowly into the infield. The batter then attempts to reach first base before the pitcher, catcher, or third or first baseman can throw him out at first. If the batters bunts the ball into foul territory, it is called a strike, just as is a normal foul. However, if the batter has two strikes against him and bunts the ball foul, the ball is called a strike, and the batter is out. (If the foul in this situation were not a bunt, it would not be called a strike.)

A *sacrifice bunt* is a bunt that advances a runner safely to the next base, but puts the batter out. A *sacrifice fly* also advances a runner at the expense of the batter. It is called when the batter hits a fly to the outfield which is caught for an out, but the runner on third tags up (retouches the base) and scores. Neither sacrifice is listed as a time at bat for the batter and does not affect his batting average.

An *infield fly* is a fly ball that can be caught easily by an infielder. It can occur only when the team at bat has less than two outs and when there are runners on first and second or on all the bases. The ball must be a fly, not a line drive or bunt. The umpire must call the infield fly rule loud and clear as soon as possible. Raise your hand and yell, "Infield fly rule, batter is out if fair." In this situation, runners advance at their own risk. If the ball goes foul, the call is ignored, and it is counted as any foul. This rule is meant to prevent infielders from dropping fly balls on purpose in order to get a double or triple play.

A *fly ball* is a batted ball that rises a significant distance off the ground. A *line drive*, on the other hand, travels parallel or close to the ground for most of its flight and is usually hit very hard. A *ground ball* is a hit that bounces off the ground and usually is handled by an infielder. It is neither a fly nor a line drive.

A runner *overslides* or *overruns* a base when, after touching the base to which he was advancing, his momentum carries him past the base so that he loses contact with it.

The *pitcher* is the player who delivers the ball to the batter. The *pitch* is the ball thrown legally to the batter. A *feint*, used by a pitcher to deceive a runner, is a movement that imitates the start of a pitch or throw to a base. The pitcher's *pivot foot* is the foot he uses to push off from the pitcher's plate. A *balk* is an illegal act committed by a pitcher when a runner is on base. Each base runner is allowed to advance one base when a balk is called. An *illegal pitch* is a pitch delivered by a pitcher who does not have his foot on the pitcher's plate or a *quick-return pitch*. A quick-return pitch is a pitch made immediately after the catcher returns the ball to the pitcher and before the batter is ready to receive it. If runners are on base, an illegal pitch is ruled a balk.

An umpire calls "play ball" to start a ballgame or to restart it after time has been called. An umpire's decision on a play is called a *play ruling*. A *double play* is a play that puts out two players. A *force play* occurs when a batter forces the runner on base to advance to the next base. A *force-out* is an out that results from a force play.

A *squeeze play*, a gamble by the offensive team, is one of the most exciting plays in baseball. The squeeze play occurs with a runner on third. As the pitcher goes into his windup, the runner on third breaks for home, and the batter bunts the ball in an attempt to allow him to score.

An *appeal play* occurs when the fielding team spots a base running infraction and calls it to the attention of the umpire, who (according to the rules) has ignored it. The fielding team tries to put the runner out after the play is over; this attempt must be made with a live ball and before the next pitch. For example: a runner misses touching first on his way to third after hitting a triple. The fielding team calls the miss to the attention of the umpire and "appeals" the play either by stepping on first base or by tagging the runner. As an umpire, you should watch for the missed base, but you should not call it *unless* the fielding team makes an appeal.

A *put-out* occurs when a fielder retires a batter or runner. A *tag-out* is made when a fielder, holding the ball in his hand or glove, tags a runner who is not touching base. A *throw-out* is an out made by a throw to first base to retire the batter or by a throw to any base to which a runner is forced. A *strike-out* results when the pitcher gets a third strike on a batter.

The goal in baseball is to score more runs than the opposing team. A *run* is scored when a runner legally advances around all four bases. The *runner* is a player on the team at bat who has finished his turn at bat but who has not been put out. The runner occupies a base and tries to advance progressively around the bases, eventually scoring a run by ending up back at home plate. The *batter-*

runner is the player who is at bat or has finished his turn at bat but has not yet touched first base or been put out.

If a runner advances to another base (except first) without the aid of an error, hit, or fielder's choice, it is considered a *stolen base*. The runner breaks for the base as soon as the pitcher goes into his windup, and to be successful must arrive at the base before the catcher throws the ball to the fielder covering the base. A *double or triple steal* occurs when two or three players steal on the same play.

The *strike zone* is the area directly above home plate which is between the batter's armpits and the top of his knees when he is in his natural batting stance. The umpire decides exactly what constitutes the batter's natural batting stance.

The umpire calls "time" when he wants to stop the game for any reason. A player is charged with a *time at bat* when he enters the batter's box, with several exceptions. The batter is not charged with a time at bat if he (1) makes a sacrifice hit, (2) gets hit with a pitched ball, (3) gets walked, (4) is replaced by a pinch hitter before he has two strikes against him, (5) is replaced by a pinch hitter after he has two strikes but the pinch hitter does not strike out, or (6) advances to first base because of interference by a fielder.

A *wild pitch* is a pitch that cannot be handled by the catcher with reasonable effort.

Situation: In a nonconference high school game, Notre Dame of Niles is playing at Maine East. It is the bottom of the seventh,

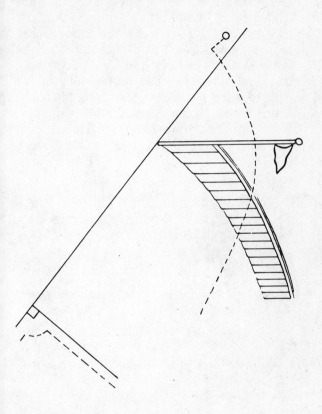

Ball passes over the fence fair, but
curves and lands in foul territory.
A home run.

and Maine East is losing 3-0. The bases are loaded, and Maine East's clean-up batter is at the plate. On the first pitch, the batter cracks a deep fly ball to left field, that sails over the fence in fair territory and then curves past into foul territory. The umpire allows the runs to score, despite protests from the Notre Dame coach. Maine East wins 4-3.

Ruling: The umpire is correct. The ball was fair when it went over the fence. (See Figure 3-1.)

4

Substituting, Coaching, Bench and Field Conduct, Charged Conferences

RULE 3

Section 1.—Substituting

ART. 1 . . . After the umpire HAS RE-CEIVED THE OFFICIAL LINE-UP CARD prior to the game, the player listed as pitcher shall pitch until the first opposing batter has been put out or has advanced to first base. In any other case, a SUBSTITUTE may replace a player of his team when the ball is dead and time has been called. The substitute or his coach shall report to the chief umpire by stating his name, shirt number, the name of the player he is replacing in the batting order and the position he will play in the field.

The substitute becomes a player when he or a team representative reports the substitute's name to the umpire in chief.

PENALTY—For illegal substitution, such substitute shall be disqualified for the duration of the game. The batting out of order rule will also apply if discovered by the defense or the umpire in chief.

PLAY (1)—S¹ replaces B³ who is third in the batting order. Is it necessary that S¹ bat in third place? RULING: Yes.

PLAY (2)—S¹ replaces B¹. Before or after he enters the batter's box, the pitcher is replaced. S¹ is then replaced. RULING: Legal.

ART. 2 . . . A SUBSTITUTE or player who replaces a pitcher whose team is not at bat shall pitch to the first opponent to bat against him until that batter has advanced to first base (including an intentional base on balls), or has been put out or until there has been a third out. To insure that the requirements of this article be fulfilled, the umpire will deny any coach-defensive player conference which will violate it. EXCEPTION: If a pitcher is incapacitated or guilty of flagrant unsportsmanlike conduct this rule is ignored.

ART. 3 . . . ANY OF THE STARTING PLAYERS may withdraw and reenter once, including the designated hitter, provided such player occupies the same batting position whenever he is in the lineup. The pitcher is governed by the provisions of Article 2 above. A substitute who is withdrawn may not reenter.

ART. 4 . . . A HITTER MAY (IT IS NOT MANDATORY) BE DESIGNATED for any one starting player (not just pitchers) and all subsequent substitutes for that player in the game. A Designated Hitter for said player must be selected prior to the start of the game, and his name must be included in the lineup cards presented to the umpire in chief and to the official scorer. IT IS NOT MANDATORY THAT A TEAM USE A DESIG-

NATED HITTER, but failure to declare such a hitter prior to the game precludes the use of a designated hitter in that game. If a pinch hitter or pinch runner for the designated hitter is used, the role of the designated hitter is terminated for the duration of the game. The designated hitter may reenter as any other player under the reentry rule. A starting player for whom the designated hitter bats may pinch hit or pinch run for the designated hitter, but if this happens, it shall terminate the designated hitter role for the remainder of the game. The designated hitter may be used defensively, but must continue to bat in the same position in the batting order as determined prior to the game. Once a designated hitter assumes a defensive position, this move shall terminate the designated hitter role for the remainder of the game. A DESIGNATED HITTER IS "LOCKED" INTO THE BATTING ORDER. No multiple substitutions may be made that will alter the batting rotation of the Designated Hitter.

Section 2.—Coaching

ART. 1 . . . ONE PLAYER, coach, or eligible substitute may occupy each COACH'S BOX while his team is at bat. He shall be in the uniform of his team. He may address baserunner or batter.

ART. 2 . . . A COACH shall not interfere by: (a) holding or pushing a runner in such a way as to assist him in returning to or leaving a base; nor (b) while third base is occupied, running toward home base on or near the base line in such a way as to draw a throw.

ART. 3 . . . ANY PERSON connected with
the team at bat shall not be near a base for
which a runner is trying so that a fielder may
be confused; nor shall he fail to vacate any
area needed by a fielder in his attempt to put
out a batter or runner. If a thrown live ball
accidentally touches a base coach, who is in
the coach's box, or a pitched or thrown ball
touches the umpire, the ball remains alive.

PENALTY—(Art. 2-3): For interference—In Art. 2, runner is out. In Art. 3,
batter or runner may be out as in 8-4-2-b
and 7-3-5.

Section 3. Bench and Field Conduct

ART. 1 . . . A COACH, player, substitute,
attendant, or other bench personnel shall not:
a. Deliberately throw a bat or helmet; or
b. Call "time" or use any command or
   commit any act for the purpose of trying
   to cause the opposing pitcher to balk; or
c. Use word or act to incite or try to incite
   spectators to demonstrations, or use pro-
   fanity or remarks which reflect upon opposing player, umpire or spectator; or
d. Enter the area behind the catcher while
   the opposing pitcher and catcher are in
   their positions.
e. Use amplifiers or bullhorns on the bench
   or on the field during the course of the
   game; or
f. Maliciously run into a fielder who has the
   ball.
g. Have any subject in his possession in the
   coach's box other than a scorebook which

shall be used for scorekeeping purposes only; or

h. **Be outside the vicinity** of the designated dugout (bench) or bullpen area if not a batter, runner, on-deck batter, in the coach's box or one of the nine players on defense.

PENALTY: In (a), (b), (f), umpire shall banish the offender from the field. Failure to comply shall result in game being forfeited. However, in (c), (d), (e), (g), and (h), if the offense is judged to be of a minor nature, the umpire may warn the offender and then disqualify him if he repeats the offense.

Section 4.—Charged Conferences

ART. 1 . . . Each team when on defense may be granted not more than three charged conferences during a seven-inning game, without penalty, to permit a coach or his representative to confer with a defensive player or players. In any extra inning game, each team shall be permitted one charged conference each inning while on defense without penalty. The number of charged conferences permitted is not cumulative. A request for time for this purpose may be made by a coach, player, substitute or an attendant. Time granted for an obviously incapacitated player shall not constitute a charged conference nor shall a conference be charged whenever the pitcher is removed as pitcher.

PENALTY: For any charged conference in excess of three in a seven inning game, or for any charged conference in

excess of one in each extra inning, the pitcher must be removed as pitcher for duration of game.

ART. 2 . . . Each team when on offense may be granted not more than one charged conference per inning to permit the coach or any of that team's personnel to confer with base runners and/or the batter. The umpire shall deny any subsequent offensive team requests for charged conferences.

INTERPRETATION
Substituting

A substitute can only enter the game and become a player when he or a team representative—usually the coach—reports him in to the umpire in chief. (In some leagues the substitution is reported to the official scorer.) For the substitution to become official, the umpire in chief must be told the substitute's name, shirt number, the name of the player he is replacing in the batting order, and the position he will play in the field. If an illegal substitution is made, that substitute is disqualified for the remainder of the game. It is common courtesy, although not required, for a coach to report substitutions to the coach of the opposing team.

If a substitute or player already in the game replaces the pitcher when the team is in the field, the new pitcher must pitch until the first batter he faces reaches first base or gets put out, or until there is a third out. There are two exceptions to this rule: if the pitcher is injured so severely that he cannot play any longer (determined by the umpire in

chief) or if the pitcher is guilty of unsportsmanlike conduct and is ejected from the
game.

Situation: In a Missouri Valley Conference
game, Indiana State University is hosting
Wichita State University. In the bottom of
the fifth inning, the Indiana State coach asks
for time, goes out to the mound, and removes
his pitcher even though there are two outs
and a runner on first. On the very first pitch
by the new pitcher the runner breaks for
second base and is thrown out by the catcher
to retire the side. At the start of the next
inning, the Indiana State coach substitutes
another new pitcher.

Ruling: This is legal, since the first relief
pitcher was in the game during a third out.

Any starting player, including the designated hitter, may leave the game and reenter one time, but must bat in the same spot. If
a substitute is taken out of the game, he is
through and may not reenter.

Designated Hitters

Each team may use a designated hitter who
may bat for one spot in the batting order. He
must be selected before the game, and his
name must be on the lineup card. The designated hitter may not play a defensive position. If he does, or if a pinch-runner or pinch-
batter is used to replace him, then the role of
designated hitter is terminated for the remainder of the game. Also, the designated
hitter is "locked" into the batting order.

The designated hitter is used for a variety
of reasons. The manager may want to rest a

player by allowing him to bat and not play the field. The manager may have the designated hitter bat in the pitcher's place in the batting order to keep the pitcher fresh. The most common use for the designated hitter, however, is simply to put more offensive punch into the lineup. Consequently, the weakest hitter—usually the pitcher, but not always—is replaced by the designated hitter in the batting order.

Situation: Louisiana State University has only ten players available during a game against the University of Mississippi. One of the Louisiana State University players is used as the designated hitter, batting fourth in the lineup. In the third inning, the LSU second baseman, who bats seventh in the lineup, is hit on the hand with a line drive and has to leave the game. The coach replaces him at second base with the designated hitter. Does the new second baseman bat in the seventh spot or in the fourth spot?

Ruling: He bats in the fourth spot because he is "locked" into the batting order. The player who did not bat before (probably the pitcher) now bats in the seventh spot.

Coaching

A coach's functions are to encourage his team and to provide the players with instruction. One coach, or an eligible substitute, may occupy each coach's box along the third and first base lines. The coach must wear his team uniform, and he may talk to his players on the bases or at bat.

A coach may not interfere with one of his

players by pushing, holding, or physically helping him to get to a base faster. In other words, when there is a play in the making, the coach must keep his hands off his base runner. A coach is not allowed to try to distract a fielder by confusing him. For the third base coach, this includes running down the line as if to draw a throw when there is a man on third.

If a ball happens to touch a coach when he is in the coach's box, the ball remains alive. This is also true when a thrown ball hits an umpire.

Bench and Field Conduct

Managers and coaches are responsible for keeping their personnel under control during a ball game. Baseball is a game of skill and strategy and should be played without unsportsmanlike behavior. Umpires should penalize such behavior accordingly. Any person associated with a baseball team is not permitted to:

1. Deliberately throw a bat or helmet.

2. Purposefully distract an opposing pitcher, batter, or any other opponent. (Example: Shouting at the pitcher to cause him to balk.)

3. Try to rile the crowd to encourage verbal abuse of an opposing player or umpire.

4. Enter the area behind the catcher to view the pitcher's tosses before an inning or during the game.

5. Use amplifiers, bullhorns, or whistles on the bench or on the field during the game.

6. Run into a fielder who has the ball in order to hurt him.

7. Have any object in the coach's box other than a scorebook.

8. Be outside of the dugout area unless he is a batter, runner, on-deck batter, pitcher in the bullpen, or one of the nine players on the field.

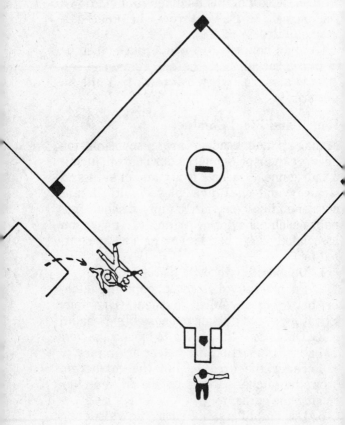

A coach or teammate may not physically assist a player in the base path.

Umpires should penalize the first two violations with ejection from the game and issue warnings for the others.

Situation: The University of Iowa Hawkeyes are playing a nonconference away game against their state rival, the Iowa State Cyclones. The Hawkeyes lead 4-2 in the bottom of the seventh, but Iowa State is threatening. There are two outs and men at first and third. An Iowa State batter hits a long fly ball which falls between the left and center fielders. The runner on third base scores easily, but as the runner on first rounds third base, he slips and falls down. The Cyclone coach helps his player up, allowing him to score before the ball reaches the catcher. Is this legal?

Ruling: No. The umpire calls the runner who fell out. All action that took place before that point remains valid. The run counts, and the batter is credited with a double. Iowa wins the game, 4-3.

Charged Conferences

ON DEFENSE.   Each team on defense may have up to three charged conferences in a seven-inning game. In extra-inning games, one extra charged conference is allowed for each extra inning. Conferences not used during the regular seven innings or during each extra inning are not cumulative. If time is granted for an injury or equipment problem or if the pitcher is removed as pitcher, no conference charge will be made. Any coach or player may request time out for a conference.

ON OFFENSE.   On offense a team may have one charged conference per inning. The umpire does not allow any other requests for charged conferences.

5

Starting and Ending Game

RULE 4
Section 1.—Starting the Game

ART. 1 ... BEFORE GAME TIME, the home team and then the visiting team shall deliver their respective batting orders to the umpire. The umpire shall then permit inspection by both captains or coaches and announce the battery for each team. The substitution regulations as in Rule 3 are then in effect.

ART. 2 ... The HOME COACH shall decide whether the grounds and other conditions are suitable for starting the game.

NOTE: After the game starts, the umpires are sole judges as to whether conditions are fit for play, and as to whether conditions are suitable for starting the second game of a scheduled double-header (two games between the same teams during the same day).

ART. 3 ... If there are unusual conditions, such as spectators or obstacles too near the playing field, the home coach shall propose special GROUND RULES. If sanctioned by the visiting team, these shall be in force. If the teams cannot agree, the umpires shall formulate ground rules. All special rules shall be announced.

ART. 4 . . . THE VISITING TEAM shall be the first to take its term at bat. On a neutral field or by agreement, either team may be designated as Home Team.

ART. 5 . . . THE GAME BEGINS when the umpire calls "Play ball" at scheduled game time.

Section 2.—Ending a Game

ART. 1 . . . A REGULATION INTERSCHOLASTIC GAME consists of seven innings (turns at bat) unless extended because of a tie score (Art. 6) or unless shortened because: the home team needs none of its half of the seventh or only a fraction of it (Art. 2); or because of weather, darkness, or similar conditions (Art. 4). It is not regulation game if a team does not have nine players in its lineup throughout the game and the game is forfeited to the opponents by the umpire in chief.

ART. 2 . . . THE GAME ENDS when the visiting team completes its half of the seventh inning, provided its runs are fewer than the number scored by the home team in six innings.

NOTE: By state association adoption, a game may end after five innings when a team is ten or more runs behind and has completed its term at bat.

ART. 3 . . . If it is necessary for the HOME TEAM to use its last inning (or its extra inning after a tie), both the inning and the game end immediately when the winning run is scored before the third player is out (see 9-1-1). EXCEPTION: If the last batter in any game hits a home run over the fence or into a stand, all runners and the batter score and the batter is credited with a home run. Each runner, including the batter-runner, should move along the proper base lines to home plate even though an incidental failure to touch such is ignored because the bases were awarded when ball became dead. See penalty exception in 8-2.

PLAY—In the last inning R^1 is on third and R^2 on second when B^3 hits and advances to third. RULING: If score was tied, only the score by R^1 counts and B^3 is credited with a single. If two runs are needed to win, both scores count, and B^3 is credited with a double.

ART. 4 . . . IF DARKNESS, rain or other cause interferes with play so that the game is called (ended) by the umpire, it is a regulation game: (a) if five full innings have been played, or if the team second at bat has scored an equal or greater number of runs in four or four and a fraction terms at bat than the opponent has scored in five terms at bat; or (b) if play has gone beyond five full innings.

In (b), if the game is called when the teams have not had an equal number of completed terms at bat, the score shall be the same as it was at the end of the last completed inning, except that if the home team, in their half of the incomplete inning, scores a run (or runs) which equals or exceeds the opponent's score, the final score shall be as recorded when the game is called.

NOTE: By state association adoption any game terminated by artificial light failure or an automatic sprinkler system shall be considered a suspended game and shall be continued from point of suspension at a later time, unless the teams mutually agree otherwise.

PLAY (1)—Sixth inning begins with H.6-V.5. Visitors score one run in their half of the sixth to tie the score. Game is called when only one or two are out in the last half of the sixth and: (a) H has not scored; or (b) H has scored one run. RULING: In (a), the score reverts to H.6-V.5. In (b), the final score is H.7-V.6.

PLAY (2)—Sixth inning begins with score H.5-V.6. Visitors do not score in their half of the sixth. Game is called when only one or two are out in the last half of the sixth and: (a) H has not scored; or (b) H has scored one run. RULING: In (a), final score is H.5-V.6. In (b), final score is H.6-V.6.

ART. 5 . . . IF GAME IS CALLED before completion of the number of innings and conditions as specified in Article 4, the umpire shall declare the contest "no game."

NOTE: By state association adoption such called game shall be considered a suspended game and shall be continued from point of suspension at a later time. The lineup and batting order of each team shall be exactly the same as the lineup and batting order at the moment of suspension, subject to the rules governing the game.

ART. 6 . . . IF THE SCORE IS TIED when seven innings have been completed, play shall continue until one team has scored more runs than the other in an equal number of full innings or until the game is ended as in Article 3.

IF A REGULATION CALLED GAME has a tie score when ended as in Article 4, it is a tie game. Batting and fielding records are counted but the game is not counted in computing percentages of games won and lost except when Note 1 of this article is adopted.

NOTE 1: By state association adoption a regulation called game with a tie score shall be counted as a half game won and a half game lost for each team.

NOTE 2: By state association adoption in tournament play, any suspended game shall be continued from point of suspension at a later time as outlined in 4-2-5—Note above.

Section 3.—Forfeited Game

ART. 1 . . . A game shall be FORFEITED to the offended team by the umpire when a team:

a. Is five minutes late in appearing or in beginning play after the umpire calls "Play ball" at scheduled game time. This may be set aside if the umpire considers the delay unavoidable; or

b. Refuses to continue play after the game has started; or

c. Delays more than one minute in resuming play after the umpire calls "Play ball" or in obeying the umpire's order to remove a player for violation of the rules; or

d. Persists in tactics designed to delay or shorten the game; or

e. Willfully and persistently violates any one of the rules after being warned by the umpire; or

f. Cannot provide nine players to finish the game; or

g. On its home field, fails to comply with the umpire's order to put the field in condition for play.

NOTE: The time limits are somewhat elastic. It is not necessary for the umpire to use a watch.

ART. 2 . . . SCORE OF A FORFEITED GAME is 7 to 0. If the game is forfeited after the number of innings required for a regulation game (as in ART. 4 of Sec. 2), and the offending team is behind, the score remains as recorded. If the offending team is leading, the score shall be 7 to 0. All individual and team averages shall be included in the official records, except that no pitcher shall be credited with a victory or charged with a loss in such game if it is not a regulation game.

Section 4.—Protested Game

ART. 1 . . . IT IS OPTIONAL on the part of a state association and other allied groups as to whether protests are permitted. When protests are submitted to organizations which do allow the filing, such protest must be submitted as described in Rule 10-2-2-i.

INTERPRETATION
Starting the Game

Before the game starts, the team captains and coaches give their batting orders to the umpire in chief. The umpire checks them over and then announces the battery (pitcher and catcher) for each team.

If the playing grounds are in questionable condition, the home coach decides whether the area is suitable for starting the game. Once the game begins, however, the umpires are the only ones allowed to decide whether or not conditions are fit for play. In the case of unusual playing conditions, the home coach submits special ground rules to the umpires for approval by the visiting coach. If they are not accepted, the umpire will issue his own special ground rules, and they will be final.

If the game is played on a neutral field, the teams must be assigned home or visitor. The visiting team always bats first at the start of each inning.

The game officially starts when the umpire calls, "Play ball."

Ending the Game

A regulation game lasts seven innings, unless extended because of a tie score, or unless it is shortened because of darkness or inclement weather. A team must have nine players in the lineup throughout the contest for it to be a regulation game.

The game ends when the visiting team completes its half of the seventh inning, provided it has fewer runs at that point than the home team. Some leagues use a "slaughter rule"—the game is over if a team is winning by ten or more runs after five innings of play. If the home team needs to use its time at bat in the seventh inning or in extra innings, both the inning and the game end when the winning run scores. Thus, the game can end before the third batter is out.

If darkness, rain, or some other cause interferes with play, the games must be ended by the umpire. A game is considered a regulation game only if one of these requirements is met:

1. Five full innings have been played.

2. The home team has scored an equal or greater number of runs in four innings or four and a fraction innings than the opponent has scored in five innings.

3. The game has gone beyond five full innings. If the game is called when the teams have not had an equal number of completed turns at bat, then the score reverts back to the last completed inning with one exception. If the home team's score equals or exceeds the visiting team's total when the game is called, the final score is recorded when the game is called.

If the umpire ends the game before any of these requirements are met, it is called "no game." In some leagues, these games are considered suspended and are continued at a later time. They are picked up from the exact point of play at which they were stopped. Both the batting order and lineups remain the same as they were in the previous game.

If the game is tied after seven innings,

extra innings are played until one team scores more runs than the other. If a regulation called game ends in a tie score, it is considered a tie game. A tie game is counted in the league standings as a half win and a half loss. If at all possible, umpires should avoid ending games that are tied. Batting and fielding percentages both count toward individual records after a tie game.

Forfeited Game

There are several reasons why a game may end as a forfeit:

1. A team shows up too late for a game.

2. A team delays too long to continue play after the start of a game.

3. A team delays too long in removing a player after he has been ejected from the game.

4. A team intentionally tries to delay or to speed up a game.

5. A team is without nine players at any point during the game.

6. On their home field, a team fails to obey the umpire's order to get the field ready for play.

In all these situations, the umpire should use discretion when debating whether or not to forfeit a game. The umpire should be flexible and only forfeit a game if it seems completely necessary. It should be a last-resort measure.

When a game is forfeited, the score is recorded as 7-0, with one exception. If the game is forfeited after the number of innings required for a regulation game and the offending team is behind, the score remains as it stands. All individual and team averages are included in the official record. The only exception is that no pitcher is credited with a win or loss.

Protested Game

In some leagues, protests are allowed. Each organization has its own rules and regulations on protests. If a team wants to protest a game, the umpire should allow it, providing it is not a protest on a judgment call. The proper steps should be followed, and the umpire should send a report of the questionable situation to the league directors.

6

Dead Ball and Suspension of Play

RULE 5

Section 1.—Dead Ball

ART. 1 . . . BALL BECOMES DEAD IMMEDIATELY when:

a. **A pitch touches:** a batter or his clothing as in 8-1-1-d; or a runner as in 8-3-1-a; or

NOTE: The ball becomes dead even though the batter strikes at it. For right to advance to first base, see Rule 8-1-1-d.

b. The ball is **illegally batted** (7-3) or is intentionally struck with the bat as in 8-4-1-c; or

c. **Any batted ball** which: while on or over foul ground touches any object other than the ground or any person other than a fielder; or goes directly from the bat to the catcher's protector, mask or person without first touching the catcher's glove or hand; or becomes an uncaught foul; or

d. **There is interference** by a runner or a retired runner as in 3-3-1-f, 8-4-1-a, c or g or 8-4-2-b, f or i; or by any person as in 3-2-2 or 3; or

81

e. **A fair ball** which is on or over fair ground touches a runner or an umpire before touching any fielder and before passing any fielder other than the pitcher; or touches a runner after passing through or by an infielder and another infielder could have made a play on the ball; or touches a spectator; or goes over or through or wedges in the field fence; or

f. **A pitch or any other thrown ball** is touched by a spectator, or when a pitch or any other thrown ball is intentionally touched by a non-participating squad member, or goes **into a stand** or players' bench (even if it rebounds to the field), or over or through or wedges in the field fence as in 8-3-3-c or -d, or lodges in an umpire's equipment; or

g. The **umpire handles a live ball or calls** "Time" for inspecting the ball or for any other reason, including items in Section 2.

h. **A fielder,** after catching a fair or foul ball (fly or line drive), leaves the field of play by stepping with both feet or by falling into a bench, dugout, stand, bleacher, or over any boundary or barrier such as a fence, rope, chalk line, or a pregame determined imaginary boundary line; or

i. Any personnel connected with the offensive team calls "Time" or use any other command or commits an act for the purpose of trying to cause the opposing pitcher to balk.

PLAY—A thrown ball touches a bat boy, substitute or attendant or equipment lying on the ground. Does ball become dead? RUL-

ING: Unless there are ground rules to the contrary, ball remains alive except when there is intended hindrance.

ART. 2 . . . BALL BECOMES DEAD AT TIME INFRACTION OCCURS if infraction is not ignored when:

a. **A balk is committed;** exception 6-2-5 Penalty; or

b. **There is interference by a batter;** exception 7-3-5 Penalty; or

c. **A catcher or any fielder interferes** with a batter, exception 8-1-1-e; or interferes with the ball through use of detached player equipment, exception 8-1-1-e, 8-3-3; or

d. **Umpire interferes** with catcher who is attempting to throw out a runner.

ART. 3 . . . BALL BECOMES DEAD WHEN TIME IS TAKEN TO MAKE AN AWARD when a catcher or any fielder illegally obstructs a runner (exception 8-3-2) or when an intentional base on balls is to be awarded.

ART. 4 . . . AFTER DEAD BALL, the ball becomes alive when it is held by the pitcher in a legal pitching position and the umpire calls "Play ball" and gives beckoning hand signal.

Section 2.—Suspension of Play

ART. 1 . . . "TIME" shall be called by the umpire and play is suspended when:

a. The ball **becomes dead** as in Art. 1, 2 or 3 of Sec. 1 or

b. He considers the **weather or ground** condition unfit for play; or

NOTE: After thirty minutes, he may declare the game ended.

c. A player, bench personnel, or spectator is **ordered from the grounds** or player is ordered to secure protective equipment; or

d. An umpire or **player is incapacitated**, except that if injury occurs during a live ball, time shall not be called until no further advance or put-out is possible; or

e. A player or coach requests "**Time**" for a substitution, conference with the pitcher, or for similar cause; or

f. He suspends play for **any other cause**, including an award of a base after an infraction, inspection of the ball or the ending of a half-inning as in 2-7-2.

ART. 2 . . . WHILE THE BALL IS DEAD, no action by a player during that time can cause him to be put out nor may a runner advance or return to a base he failed to touch during a live ball, except that any runner may be awarded a base or bases, or an act which occurred before the ball became dead as in 8-1-2 or 8-3.

PLAY (1)—R^1 is attempting to steal second when there is a balk which is not followed by a pitch. R^1 reaches second base after the balk. RULING: Ball becomes dead when the balk occurs. R^1 is not entitled to a stolen base since he could not advance during dead ball. He is awarded second as penalty for the balk.

PLAY (2)—With R^1 at third, R^2 at second, and R^3 at first, ball batted by B^4 hits R^2. R^1 runs home and R^3 is tagged on his way to second. RULING: Ball became dead when it hit R^2. R^2 is out and B^4 is also out if the umpire believes the interference by R^3 may have prevented a double play involving B^4. R^1 returns to third. If B^4 is not declared out, R^3 is awarded second since the base where he was at time of the pitch is occupied. If B^4 is declared out, R^3 returns to first.

INTERPRETATION
Dead Ball

During a dead ball situation, all action ceases. No player can be put out or advance on the base paths, except to be awarded a base for an infraction by the defensive team. Dead ball situations can be classified in two ways:

1. When the ball is declared dead immediately.

2. When the ball is declared dead after the completion of a play. This is called a delayed dead ball, and is signaled when the umpire shouts, "Time!" The delayed dead ball usually follows an infraction of the rules by either team during play.

Here is how the ball becomes dead immediately:

1. A pitch hits a batter. If this happens, the batter is awarded first base. As umpire, you should ignore this call if you feel the batter did not try to avoid being hit by the pitch. If a batter swings at a pitch and it hits him, the ball is considered dead but the batter is not awarded first base.

2. When the batter's bat touches the ball twice. If this is intentional, the batter is ruled out.

3. On an illegally batted ball. Example:

The batter hits the ball when he has one foot out of the batter's box. In this case, he is out, and all runners return to their original bases.

4. On an uncaught foul ball.

5. When interference is called on a runner. As umpire, you should call the runner out. If in your judgment the interference prevented a double play, you also should declare the batter-runner out.

6. When a coach or any other team personnel is called for interference.

7. When a fair ball passes over a fence in the outfield.

8. When a fair ball gets stuck in a fence. The umpire rules "dead ball" and declares a "ground rule double," unless decided upon differently before the game by umpires and coaches.

9. When a fair ball touches a runner.

10. When a spectator touches the ball.

11. When a thrown ball goes out of bounds.

12. When the umpire calls time.

13. When a fielder catches a fly ball and his momentum carries him off the playing field into an out-of-bounds area. If this happens, all the runners are allowed to advance one base, unless the catch determined the third out. In that case, the inning is over.

14. When a balk is called and a pitch hasn't been thrown.

15. When any person associated with the offensive team tries to distract the pitcher into making a balk. As umpire, you must determine whether or not to eject the offender(s) immediately or simply issue a warning for the first offense. In either case, you must

take some action, because intentional distractions are not justified.

Sometimes when a rule infraction occurs, the umpire must delay his call until he sees what type of action develops.

Example: Interference by the batter against the catcher while a runner is attempting to steal a base. If there are two outs, the batter is out immediately. If there are fewer than two outs, the umpire waits to see if the runner gets thrown out. If he does, the play stands "as is," and the interference is ignored. If the runner is safe, the umpire declares the batter out and sends the runner back to the base that he came from. This play is considered a delayed dead ball.

Here are additional delayed dead ball situations:

1. When there is an illegal pitch with no runner on base. The pitch is called a ball (even if it is in the strike zone), unless the batter gets on base.

2. When a balk is followed by a pitch. If the batter and runners all manage to advance at least one base on the pitch, then the balk is ignored. If they aren't able to advance to the next base on their own, the umpire awards them that base.

3. When there is an interference by the batter while a fielder is making a play at any base.

4. When the catcher interferes with the batter. If the batter and runner(s) don't advance at least one base on the play, the umpire should award each of them one base.

5. When a member of the fielding team

deliberately touches a fair batted ball with some part of his equipment.

Example: A player in the bullpen deliberately touches the ball in order to slow it down, enabling his own team's outfielder to retrieve it more quickly. Each runner is awarded three bases for this infraction. If the same thing occurs on a live, *thrown* ball, two bases are awarded.

6. When the umpire interferes with the catcher. In this instance, the umpire should wait and see if the runner is thrown out. If not, the runner must return to his original base.

7. When obstruction occurs. If because of obstruction a runner does not reach the base he otherwise would have reached, he is awarded the base. This applies to all baserunners affected by the obstruction. This is considered a judgment call by the umpire, and the umpires should confer among themselves when making this call.

For a dead ball to become alive, three conditions must be met:

1. The pitcher holds the ball in a legal pitching position.

2. The umpire calls, "Play ball."

3. The umpire gives the pitcher the hand signal ordering him to begin pitching. The umpire initates play only after observing that the fielders are in their positions, the catcher is in the catcher's box, the batter is in the batter's box, and the umpire himself is ready and in position to evaluate play.

Suspension of Play

In all of the previous examples, the umpire interrupts the game by calling time. He also may call time for the following circumstances:

1. The umpire decides that weather or ground conditions are unfit for play. The umpire in chief may declare a game ended if after thirty minutes of delay conditions have not improved enough for the game to resume. You always should stop a game if you sight lightning.

2. The umpire orders someone from either team or a spectator to leave the playing grounds.

3. The umpire stops the game for an injury or an equipment problem.

4. The umpire grants a request for time by either a player or coach.

5. To award a base to a runner or batter.

6. The umpire finds it necessary to stop the game for any other reason.

Situation: In Los Angeles, the UCLA Bruins are host to crosstown rival USC. The score is tied 4-4, and the game is in extra innings. UCLA has runners on second and third bases, with only one out. The Bruins' leading hitter, their first baseman, is up to bat. On the first pitch, he hits a deep fly ball toward the right field line. It is definitely foul and is falling quickly. The USC right fielder races over and on the dead run reaches down and barely spears the ball off his shoe tops. In

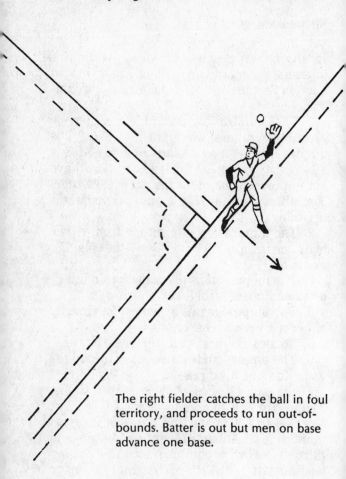

The right fielder catches the ball in foul
territory, and proceeds to run out-of-
bounds. Batter is out but men on base
advance one base.

(FIGURE 6-1)
Foul line
Out-of-bounds
line

the process, his momentum carries him out of bounds.

Ruling: The batter is out because the fielder caught the ball inbounds. However, since the fielder ran across the boundary line, the umpire correctly awards each runner one base, allowing the runner on third to score with the winning run. Final score is UCLA 5, USC 4. In this situation the right fielder would have been better off to let the ball drop for a foul ball, which would have counted as a strike. (See Figure 6-1.)

7

Pitching

RULE 6

Section 1.—Pitching Regulations

ART. 1 . . . THE PITCHER SHALL TAKE
HIS SIGN from the catcher with his pivot
foot in contact with the pitcher's plate. When
he takes his sign and his feet are in the set
position stance, the ball shall be in either his
gloved hand or his pitching hand. His pitching hand shall be down at his side or behind
his back. When he takes his sign and his feet
are in the windup position stance he is not restricted as to how he shall hold the ball. He
shall pitch while facing the batter from
either a windup position (Art. 2) or a set
position (Art. 3). His pivot foot shall be touching his plate if he uses the windup position. If
he uses the set position, his entire pivot foot
shall be on or directly in front of and in
contact with and parallel to the plate. When
he takes either a windup or set position, in
order to change to the other position he must
first step clearly backward off the pitcher's

92

plate with his pivot foot. He may then assume either position. He shall not make a quick-return pitch in an attempt to catch a batter off balance nor pitch when the catcher does not have both feet in the catcher's box.

ART. 2 . . . FOR THE WINDUP POSI-TION, the pitcher's non-pivot foot must be in any position on or behind a line extending through the front edge of the pitcher's plate. He is limited to not more than two pumps or rotations. After he starts his movement to deliver a pitch, he must continue the motion without interruption or alteration. During delivery, he may lift his non-pivot foot in a step forward, or in a step backward and a step forward, but he shall not otherwise lift either foot.

ART. 3 . . . FOR THE SET POSITION, the pitcher, before starting his delivery, shall stand with his entire non-pivot foot in front of a line extending through the front edge of the pitcher's plate with the ball in both hands in front of his body and come to a complete stop. Natural preliminary motions such as only one stretch may be made. When he elects to use the set position, he must have his entire pivot foot on or directly in front of and in contact with and parallel to the pitcher's plate and his entire non-pivot foot in front of it, before he takes the preliminary stretch with his arms. During these preliminaries and during the set position until a delivery motion occurs, the pitcher may turn on his pivot foot or lift it in a jump turn to step with the non-pivot foot toward a base while throwing or feinting as outlined in Art. 4 of Section 2 or he may lift his pivot foot on the ground clearly behind the plate, his right to throw or feint to a base is the same as that of any other infielder.

PENALTY (Art. 1, 2, 3: For illegal pitch—(a) If there is no runner, a ball is called on the batter. (b) If there is a runner, such illegal act is a balk. In either (a) or (b), umpire signals delayed dead ball provided ball is pitched, and, if ball is not pitched, he signals ball dead immediately. If batter in (a) or if batter and each runner in (b) advances at least one base because of a safe hit or error or other reason, the illegal pitch penalty is ignored.

PLAY (1)—With no runner, F^1 makes quick-return pitch or his pivot foot is not touching the plate. The pitch: (a) is through the strike zone; or (b) is struck at and missed; or (c) is hit and B^1 is thrown out at first; or (d) is hit for a safe hit or B^1 reaches first on an error or from being hit from a fourth ball. RULING: A ball in (a), (b), or (c). In (d), the penalty is automatically ignored and B^1 remains on base.

PLAY (2)—After F^1 has stretched or stopped, R^1 starts toward third. F^1 feints or throws to second or third. RULING: Legal if F^1 steps toward such base.

Art. 4 . . . EACH LEGAL PITCH shall be declared by the umpire: a strike, ball, fair or foul hit (7-2) or a dead ball (5-1-1).

NOTE: The height of the strike zone is determined by the batter's normal stance. If he crouches or leans over to make the shoulder line lower, the umpire determines height by what would be the batter's normal stance.

PLAY (1)—Pitch touches ground and bounces into strike zone. (a) B does not strike at it; or (b) strikes and misses; or (c) hits a fly ball which is caught. RULING: (a) Ball. Pitch did not enter strike zone in flight. (b) Strike. If it is third strike and catcher holds the bounced ball, B is not out unless tagged or thrown out at first. (c) Batter is out.

PLAY (2)—As F^1 winds up, R^1 advances home and is hit by the pitch. RULING: Ball becomes dead. Also, it is a ball or strike. If it is ruled a third strike, batter is out. If batter is the third out, the run does not score. Otherwise, the run scores.

ART. 5 ... WHEN A PITCHER is attempting to field a batted or thrown ball or is throwing to a base while his pivot foot is clearly off his plate, his status is that of an infielder except that if a batted ball passes but does not touch him and then strikes an umpire or a runner, the ball becomes dead for interference. See 8-3-3-d and 8-4-2-f.

Section 2.—Infractions by Pitcher
A PITCHER SHALL NOT:

ART. 1 ... DEFACE THE BALL nor deliver a defaced ball. Illegal acts include:
a. **Applying a foreign** substance to it;
b. **Spitting on ball** or glove,
c. **Rubbing** it on glove, clothing or person if the act defaces the ball;
d. **Discoloring** it with dirt; or
e. **Delivering** "shine ball," "spit ball," "mud

ball," or "emery ball."

f. **Bringing the pitching hand** in contact with the mouth without distinctly wiping off his pitching hand before it touches the ball.

NOTE: Under umpire supervision, pitcher may dry his hands by use of a finely meshed cloth bag of powdered rosin. He may rub the ball with bare hands to remove any extraneous coating.

PENALTY: For defacing ball—Pitcher may be removed from the game. If such defaced ball is pitched, it is an illegal pitch with penalty as for 6-1.

ART. 2 . . . DELAY THE GAME. This includes:

a. Throwing to any **player other than the batter,** when the batter is in his box, unless it is an attempt to retire a runner.

b. Consuming time as the result of the **coach or his representative conferring with a defensive player or players** after being charged with three conferences as outlined in 3-4-1.

c. With the bases unoccupied, failure to pitch within **twenty seconds** after there has been a reasonable time for him to receive the ball after the last pitch. EXCEPTION: At the beginning of each inning or when a pitcher is replaced during an inning, the pitcher may "warm up" by using not more than eight throws to a player unless umpire authorizes more throws because of an injury or inclement weather. Umpire shall suspend play and the batter shall remain out of his box.

d. **Any other act** which causes undue delay.

NOTE: If pitcher justifiably steps off the plate as for wiping dust or sweat from his eyes, umpire shall call time. Consumption of time for conference between catcher or coach and pitcher is permissible within reason. Repeated delays to make the batter nervous should be penalized.

PENALTY: For delay—The pitcher shall be removed from the game in (a) after warning and, in (b), the pitcher shall be replaced as pitcher, for the duration of the game. In (c) a ball shall be called, and in (d) a ball shall be called if there is no runner and a balk if there is a runner.

ART. 3 . . . INTENTIONALLY THROW close to a batter's head.

PENALTY: For throwing at batter— Disqualification. In case of doubt, umpire may first warn pitcher.

PLAY—F[1] attempts to drive B away from home base by throwing "duster" close to his head. RULING: If B is in normal position with head over batter's box, umpire shall warn or disqualify F[1] B is not protected while leaning over home base.

ART. 4 . . . BALK. If there is a runner or runners, any of the following acts by a pitcher while he is touching the pitcher's plate is a balk.

a. **Any feint** toward batter or **first base** or any dropping of the ball (even though accidental).

b. **Failing to step** with the non-pivot foot directly toward a base (occupied or unoccupied) when throwing or feinting there in an attempt to put out, or drive back a runner; or throwing or feinting to any unoccupied base when it is not an attempt to put out or drive back a runner.

c. **Making an illegal pitch** from any position as in Section 1.

d. **Failing to pitch to the batter** in a continuous motion immediately after any movement of any part of the body such as he habitually uses in his delivery.

e. **Taking a hand off the ball** while in a set position (6-1-3) unless he pitches to the batter or throws to a base or he steps toward and feints a throw to second or third base as in Item b.

f. **Failing to pitch** to the batter when the entire **non-pivot** foot passes behind the perpendicular plane of the front edge of the pitching plate except when feinting or throwing to second base in an attempt to put out a runner.

ART. 5 . . . IT IS ALSO A BALK if there is a runner or runners and the pitcher, while he is not touching the pitcher's plate, makes any movement naturally associated with his pitch; or he places his feet on or astride the pitcher's plate, or positions himself within about five feet of the pitcher's plate without having the ball; or he delays the game from any position as in 6-2-2-a, c or d, while the ball is alive.

PENALTY: For balk—Ball becomes dead and each runner is awarded one base. EXCEPTION: If the balk is followed by a pitch which because of a hit, error or other reason, permits the batter and each other runner to advance a minimum of one base, the balk is ignored and does not cause ball to become dead. If the balk is followed by a wild throw either to a base or home base and the ball does not go into a dead ball area, each runner may advance beyond the base to which he is entitled at his own risk.

PLAY (1)—R^1 is on second with none out and B^2 has three balls and two strikes. F^1 delivers an illegal pitch such as a quick-return without a stop or one with the pivot foot off the plate. The pitch is: (a) through the strike zone and caught by F^2 or the pitch hits B^2, or (b) not through the strike zone and caught by F^2; or (c) hit by B^2 with both B^2 and R^1 advancing. RULING: In (a) and (b), the balk causes the ball to become dead immediately and balk penalty is enforced. In (c), balk penalty is ignored with advances allowed and ball remains alive.

PLAY (2)—R^1 is on third. During windup, F^1 gets dust in his eyes. RULING: F^1 must pitch or, while continuing his pitching motion, request "time." Umpire will grant it if clearly it is an emergency rather than merely an attempt to stop R^1.

INTERPRETATION
Pitching Regulations

Pitching is one of the most important aspects of the game of baseball. Consequently, the umpire should watch the pitcher carefully for correct and incorrect pitching technique.

The pitcher's pivot foot must be in contact with the pitcher's plate when he takes his sign from the catcher. He may pitch from two positions—the windup position or the set position. When pitching from the windup position, the pitcher is not restricted in how he may hold the ball. However, when pitching from the set position, he must grasp the ball either in his gloved hand or his pitching hand, and his pitching hand must be down at his side or behind his back.

In either position, the pitcher's pivot foot must remain in contact with the pitcher's plate. If he wishes to change position, he must step backward off the pitcher's plate with his pivot foot before doing so. He may not pitch to the catcher unless the catcher has both feet in the catcher's box. He also may not quick-return a pitch—pitch the ball immediately after the catcher returns it to him—attempting to catch the batter off guard. If as an umpire you spot the quick-return violation, you should do one of two things: award a ball to the batter unless he gets a hit, or if there are runners on base, call a balk and allow each to advance one base.

There are several restrictions on a pitcher in the windup position:

1. Before his windup, his non-pivot foot must be either on or behind an imaginary line that would extend along the front edge of the pitcher's plate.

2. The pitcher must use no more than two pumps before delivering the pitch.

3. Once he starts his windup, he must continue his motion without interruption until he has delivered the pitch.

When there are men on base, the pitcher

goes into the set position because it is easier to hold the runners close to their bases from this position. In the set position, the restrictions on the pitcher are:

1. His non-pivot foot must be in front of the imaginary line which extends along the front edge of the pitcher's plate.

2. The pivot foot must be in front of and in contact with the pitcher's plate.

3. When going into his motion, the pitcher must come to a complete stop, with his hands in front of his body.

4. The pitcher may turn on his pivot foot, as long as he throws to the base he is stepping towards.

When the pitcher steps off the pitcher's plate to make a throw to a base, he is given the same status as any other fielder.

The home plate umpire calls each pitch as delivered by the pitcher—either a ball or a strike—unless, of course, the ball is hit. Then he should declare it either fair or foul.

Infractions by the Pitcher

If the pitcher defaces the ball in any of the following ways, the umpire should eject him from the game. If the defaced ball is pitched, it is treated as an illegal pitch and penalized as such.

1. He may not spit on the ball or his glove.

2. He may never apply a foreign substance to the ball.

3. If he brings his pitching hand to his mouth, he must *clearly* wipe off his hand before touching the ball again.

The pitcher may not delay the game by:

1. Throwing to any fielder ("playing catch") when the batter is in the box and ready to hit.

2. Calling a conference in addition to the three that are allowed per game.

3. Failing to pitch within twenty seconds after receiving the ball from the catcher following the previous pitch, while the bases are empty. The umpire should be flexible in judging this type of delay.

4. Any other act which the umpire judges to be a delay of game.

A new pitcher entering the game is allowed eight warm-up pitches. This rule fluctuates. If the weather is cold or if the pitcher enters the game to relieve an injured pitcher, the umpire should extend the maximum number of warm-up pitches.

The umpire should remove a pitcher from the game if he deliberately tries to throw a pitch at a player's head in an attempt to "brush him back." If, as umpire, you are in some doubt about the pitcher's intentions, you may warn him first.

A balk is an illegal act by the pitcher when at least one runner is on base. When it occurs, the umpire should award a one-base advance to each runner. In the case of a delayed call on a balk, the decision may be ignored if the batter and runners all advance at least one base on the play.

A balk occurs when the pitcher touches the pitcher's plate and then completes one of the following:

1. Feints toward the batter or first base.

2. Drops the ball.

3. Fails to step with the non-pivot foot directly facing a base when throwing or feinting.

4. Makes any illegal pitch that has been described earlier in the chapter.

5. Takes a hand off the ball while in a set position, unless he is pitching to the batter or throwing or feinting to a base.

6. Fails to pitch to the batter after his non-pivot foot passes entirely behind the perpendicular plane of the front edge of the pitcher's plate. The exception to this rule is when the pitcher is feinting or throwing to second base in an attempt to put out a runner.

The pitcher also may balk when he is not on the pitcher's plate. Again, at least one runner must be on base. This occurs when:

1. The pitcher makes a movement that resembles a part of his normal delivery.

2. The pitcher positions himself within five feet of the pitcher's plate without the ball.

3. The pitcher delays the game while the ball is still considered alive. (This situation was described earlier.)

Situation: The University of Minnesota is playing at Big Ten rival Indiana University. The Indiana pitcher is having a superb day. He has already accumulated eight strike-outs and only relinquished one walk to the first batter in the fourth inning. After observing another pitch successfully drop six inches, the Minnesota coach discovers the reason for his opponent's effective pitching. He asks the umpire to go out and check the pitcher's uniform. On both the flap of the pitcher's shoe and inside his glove, the umpire finds some petroleum jelly.

Ruling: Since the inspection was made after a pitch, it is handled in the same manner as a balk, providing the batter didn't advance and providing there were runners on base. If there were no runners, the pitch is called a ball. In either case, the pitcher is removed from the game.

After inspection, the umpire discovers petroleum jelly on the pitcher's mitt. Batter and runners advance one base; pitcher is ejected.

8
Batting

RULE 7

Section 1.—Position and Batting Order

ART. 1 . . . EACH PLAYER of the team at bat shall become the batter and shall take his position within a batter's box (on either side of home base), in the order in which his name appears on the scorecard as delivered to the umpire prior to the game (4-1). This order shall be followed during the entire game except that an entering substitute shall take the replaced player's place in the batting order. A batter is in proper order if he follows the player whose name precedes his in the lineup, even though such preceding batter may have batted out of order. An improper batter is considered to be at bat as soon as he is in the batter's box and the ball is alive. If the improper batter, his coach or teammate is first to discover batter's infraction, time may be requested and improper batter replaced by proper batter with the improper batter's ball and strike count still in effect, provided the infraction is detected before improper batter is put out, or becomes a base runner.

ART. 2 . . . AFTER THE FIRST INNING, the first batter in each inning shall be the player whose name follows that of the last batter who completed his time at bat in the preceding inning.

PENALTY: For batting out of order (Art. 1 and 2)—If the coach or player of team in the field is first to detect infraction before a legal pitch or an illegal pitch has been delivered to a succeeding batter, or prior to an intentional base on balls, and before the infielders leave the diamond if a half-inning is ending, the penalty shall apply as follows: (a) the player who should have batted shall be out with the catcher being credited with a put-out; (b) any advance by a runner (including the batter-runner) due to a wrong batter becoming a batter-runner is cancelled; (c) the player who batted out of order shall resume his proper place in the batting order with no balls or strikes even though this may cause him to become the next batter; (d) when several players bat out of order before discovery so that player's time at bat comes while he is a runner, such player remains on base but he is NOT out as a batter.

PLAY (1)—B^4 has two strikes and one ball when R^1 is thrown out to make the third out. RULING: B^4 is the first batter in the next inning with no balls or strikes.

PLAY (2)—It is the turn of B^5 to bat but B^7 erroneously bats. The error is discovered by

F^2 after B^7 has one or more balls or strikes. RULING: B^5 is out. B^6 is the next batter and he should be followed by B^7.

PLAY (3)—With R^1 on second, it is the time of B^3 to bat but B^4 erroneously bats. He hits a two-bagger and the irregularity is discovered, before a subsequent pitch, by: (a) coach of team in the field; or (b) F^4. RULING: In both (a) and (b) B^3 shall be declared out and B^4 shall bat again with no ball and strike count, and R^1 returns to second base.

PLAY (4)—With R^1 on second and R^2 on first, it is the time of B^3 to bat but B^5 erroneously bats. Before discovery of the irregularity, wrong batter B^5 hits safely. R^1 advances home. R^2 advances to second and B^5 advances to first. The irregularity is discovered by F^6 before a pitch to the next batter. RULING: B^3 is declared out. R^1 returns to second, R^2 to first and B^5 is removed from first base. It is the time of B^4 to bat and he will be followed by B^5.

PLAY (5)—It is the time of B^1 to bat but B^3 erroneously bats and: (a) hits safely; or (b) flies out to F^8. B^1 erroneously follows and walks. B^2 follows and walks. It is now the time of B^3 to bat. What is the penalty? RULING: There is no penalty. In (a), B^3 is left on base and B^4 becomes the next batter. In (b), B^3 is entitled to bat a second time since it is his normal time to bat.

Section 2.—Strikes, Balls and Hits

ART. 1 . . . A STRIKE is charged to the batter when a pitch:

a. **Enters any part of the strike zone** in flight and is not struck at; or
b. **Is struck at** and missed; or
c. **Becomes a foul** when the batter has less than two strikes; or
d. **Becomes** (even on third strike) **a foul tip** or a foul from an attempted bunt; or
e. **Is a penalty strike** because a batter delays as in 7-3-1.

ART. 2 ... A BALL is credited to the batter when a pitch is not touched by the bat and is not a strike or when there is an illegal pitch as in 6-1 Penalty (a).

ART. 3 ... A FOUL HIT OR FAIR HIT (which may be a bunt) occurs when a pitch is touched by the bat of the batter who is in his box.

Section 3.—Batting Infractions
A BATTER SHALL NOT:

ART. 1 ... DELAY the game by failing to promptly take his position in the batter's box.

PENALTY: For batter delaying game— Umpire shall direct pitcher to pitch and each such pitch, including any which does not go through the strike zone, shall be called a strike.

NOTE: After entering the box, a batter leaves it at the risk of having a strike thrown while he is out of position. The batter may request "time" if he desires to step out for a valid reason. The umpire is authorized to refuse to grant "time" if the batter repeatedly causes delay or if his leaving the box appears to be an attempt to worry the pitcher or to gain some other advantage.

ART. 2 . . . Hit the ball fair or foul while either foot is TOUCHING THE GROUND OUTSIDE batter's box.

NOTE: A "follow through" with the bat may carry one of the batter's feet outside the box so it touches the ground there as the ball is leaving the bat. It is customary for the umpire to ignore this if both feet were in legal position at the start of the swing and if it is not considered an attempt to cheat the spirit of the rule.

ART. 3 . . . DISCONCERT THE PITCHER by stepping from the box on one side of home base to the box on the other side while the pitcher is in position ready to pitch.

PLAY—B[1] has been batting right-handed. After having one or more strikes or balls, he desires to bat left-handed. RULING: He may change boxes before the pitcher is in position. It is safest for him to request "Time" for the change.

ART. 4 . . . Permit a pitched ball to TOUCH HIM while he is attempting a third strike.

PLAY—B[1] has two strikes. He strikes at the next pitch and ball strikes his forearm: (a) without touching his bat; or (b) after touching his bat. RULING: (a) B[1] is out and ball becomes dead. (b) Foul hit. Ball is dead. Not a ball or strike.

ART. 5 . . . INTERFERE WITH THE CATCHER'S fielding or throwing by stepping out of batter's box or making any other movement which hinders action at home base or by failing to make reasonable effort to vacate congested area when there is a throw to home base and there is time for the batter to move away.

PENALTY: For infraction of Art. 2, 3 and 4, batter is out and ball becomes dead immediately. For infraction of Art. 5: When two are out, batter is out. When two are not out and runner is advancing to home base, runner is out and ball is dead unless runner is tagged out in which case ball remains alive and interference is ignored. When attempt to put out runner at any other base is unsuccessful, batter is out and all runners must return to bases occupied at time of pitch.

Section 4.—A Batter Is Out as in above penalty or when:

a. He appears at bat with an illegal bat; or
b. A third strike (Section 2) is caught; or
c. His foul (other than a foul tip not a third strike) is caught by a fielder or such catch is prevented by a spectator reaching over the enclosed fence; or
d. An attempt to bunt on third strike is a foul; or
e. A third strike is not caught, provided a runner occupies first base and not more than one is out; or

   NOTE: If two are out or if no runner occupies 1st base, the batter is not out unless the third strike is caught. He is entitled to try to reach first base before being tagged out or thrown out.

f. An infield fly is declared as in 2-8-5 (when runners occupy first and second bases and before two are out).

   NOTE: The umpire calls "Infield fly if fair and batter is out." If the hit then be-

comes a foul, he reverses his decision. The batter is always out if it is an infield fly, but the ball is alive and runners may advance in the hope the fly may not be caught or they may retouch and advance after the ball is touched.

INTERPRETATION
Position and Batting

Each player in the game bats in a designated spot in the order. This order must be recorded in the scorebook and followed throughout the game, except when a substitute enters the game to replace another player. A substitute bats in the same spot in the order as the player he is replacing.

Batters must bat in the proper batting order, or a penalty is invoked. A player is considered to have batted in his proper order if he bats following the player whose name appears directly before his on the lineup card. This is so even if the preceding batter bats out of turn. Consider the following incident:

Situation: Auburn University is playing an intrastate foe, Alabama, in a Southeastern Conference battle. It is the top of the third inning, and Auburn comes to bat. The batting order for the inning should have been as follows: First, the third baseman; second, the center fielder; and third, the catcher. However, the Auburn players bat out of order. The catcher leads off the inning with a ground out. He is followed by the center fielder, who draws a walk. Then it is discovered that the team batted out of order.

Ruling: The third baseman should be declared out because he did not bat in his proper batting order. Since the center fielder was the last batter, the catcher must bat again, because he must follow the player who precedes him in the batting order. The player who bats first each inning is the player who follows the batter that made the last out during the previous inning.

Strikes, Ball and Hits

The umpire should charge a strike against the batter when:

1. The ball enters the strike zone during flight and is either swung at and missed or not swung at at all.

2. The ball is hit foul with less than two strikes in the count.

3. The ball is a foul tip, regardless of how many strikes the batter may have already.

4. The batter bunts foul, even on a third strike.

5. The batter is penalized for delaying the game.

A ball is only charged to the batter in these two cases: When the pitched ball does not touch his bat and has not been ruled a strike or the umpire rules an illegal pitch thrown by the pitcher.

Batting Infractions

A hit, fair or foul, is legal only if the batter has both feet in the batter's box. If he has one foot outside the box, it is a rules infraction, and the batter should be ruled "out."

Following is the list of batting infractions:

1. The batter delays the game by not taking his position in the batter's box. When this happens, the umpire should instruct the pitcher to pitch to the catcher anyway and call each pitch a strike, whether it enters the strike zone or not.

2. The batter tries to unnerve the pitcher by changing from one side of the plate to the other while the pitcher is in his windup. The ball becomes dead immediately, and the umpire should declare the batter out. It is legal for a batter to switch from batting right handed or left handed or vice versa before the pitcher goes into his windup. Changing batting position may be done on any ball and strike count.

3. The batter interferes with the catcher. This may be done by stepping out of the batter's box while the catcher is making a throw. Or, the batter may deliberately be in the way during a play at home plate, if there was a reasonable amount of time to move out of the way. It is up to the umpire's discretion to determine the fine line that exists between interference and legal action. When interference is ruled, the umpire makes a delayed dead ball call and penalizes the batter accordingly.

Batter is Out

In addition to some penalty calls, a batter is declared out when:

1. He appears at the plate with an illegal bat.

2. A third strike is caught.

3. A third strike is not caught, and there are one or no outs with first base occupied.

4. The umpire calls an infield fly (see Chapter 3).

Situation: In Little Rock, Arkansas, a high school pitcher set a new state record for strike-outs in one game. The young pitcher had an unbelievable total of 22 strike-outs in a seven inning game. How is this possible, since there are only 21 outs in a regulation seven inning game?

Ruling: The pitcher had three strike-outs each inning except in the fifth, when he was credited with four. On a third strike the catcher dropped the ball; by the time he retrieved it and threw it to first, the batter was ruled safe. The pitcher is credited with a strike-out in this situation and, by the way, so is the batter.

9

Base Running

RULE 8

Section 1.—When Batter Becomes a Runner

ART. 1 . . . A BATTER becomes a runner with the right to attempt to score by advancing to first, second, third, and then home base in the listed order when:

a. He hits a **fair ball** (2-8-1); or

NOTE: He becomes a runner when entitled to run.

b. He is charged with a **third strike** (see note); or

NOTE: If third strike is caught, he is out an instant after he becomes a runner.

c. **An intentional base on balls is awarded, or a fourth ball** is called by the umpire; or

d. A pitched **ball hits his person** or clothing, provided he does not strike at the ball. EXCEPTION: **If he makes no effort to avoid** being hit, or if the umpire calls the pitched ball a strike, the hitting of the

115

batter is disregarded except that the ball is dead. It is a strike or ball depending on location of the pitch; or

e. **The catcher or any infielder interferes** with him. If because of a hit, error or other reason, the batter and all other runners each advance a minimum of one base, the catcher's infraction is ignored and ball does not become dead.

ART. 2 . . . A BATTER-RUNNER IS AWARDED first base if:

a. **He is a runner** because of c, d or e or Art. 1; or

b. **His fair ball,** other than an infield fly, becomes dead as in d, e or f of 5-1-1 or c of 5-1-2 and provided a preceding runner or retired runner does not interfere in such a way as to prevent an obvious double play as in 8-4-1-g.

Unless awarded first base as above, a batter-runner is entitled to first base only if he reaches it before being tagged out or thrown out or called out; for hitting an infield fly as in 7-4-f; or as in 8-4-1.

PLAY (1)—With one out, R^1 is on second and R^2 on first. Infield fly by B^4 touches R^2 while he stands on first. RULING: B^4 is out. R^2 is not out. Ball becomes dead when it touches him.

PLAY (2)—R^1 is on first. Ball batted by B^2 strikes umpire who is between pitcher F^1 and second base. Ball is deflected to F^6. RULING: Unless F^1 touched the batted ball, it became dead when it touched the umpire. B^2 and R^1 are awarded first and second.

Section 2.—Touching, Occupying and Returning to a Base

ART. 1 . . . AN ADVANCING RUNNER shall touch first, second, third, and then home in order.

A RETURNING RUNNER shall retouch the bases in reverse order if the ball is alive. If the ball is dead, it is not necessary for him to retouch intervening bases.

ANY RUNNER WHO MISSES a base while advancing may not return to touch it after a following runner has scored.

NOTE: When an infraction is ignored, according to rule, any runner who misses the first base to which he is advancing and who is called out on appeal shall be considered as having advanced one base.

ART. 2 . . . IF A BATTED BALL (fair or foul other than a foul tip) IS CAUGHT, each base runner shall touch his base after the batted ball has touched a fielder. (See 8-4-1-b for fielder intentionally dropping ball and 8-4-2-d for runner being put out.)

ART. 3 . . . IF A BATTER-RUNNER is entitled to return to first base after overrunning it or if a runner fails to touch home base and if either such runner desires to return, he shall return immediately.

PENALTY (Art. 1, 2, 3): For failure to touch base (advancing or returning)— Runner is out if, before he returns to each untouched base, he is touched by the ball in the hand of a fielder as in 8-4-2-c, or if ball is held by a fielder on any base (including home base) the runner failed to

touch. EXCEPTIONS: Penalty is ignored if umpires failed to observe the infraction; or if an appeal is not made to them before the time of the first succeeding legal or illegal pitch or prior to an awarded intentional base on balls or before the infielders leave the diamond when a half-inning is ending; or if the untouched base is one which has been awarded the runner because ball has become dead. Also, when a runner is legally returning after a long fly has been caught, he cannot be put out by a fielder merely touching a base other than the one occupied by the runner at the time of the pitch.

PLAY (1)—R^1: (a) goes past home base but fails to touch it and makes no immediate attempt to return for the touch; or (b) R^2 slides or runs past second and fails to touch it. May runner be put out by ball holder touching the base without a tag? RULING: Yes for (a). No for (b) unless it is a force or appeal play.

PLAY (2)—R^1 is on second base. Fair hit by B^2 goes over the fence. R^1 or B^2 fails to touch one of the bases. RULING: Since ball became dead and home base is awarded both runners, failure to touch a base is ignored. However, all runners are obligated to move along the proper base lines.

ART. 4 . . . A BATTER-RUNNER WHO REACHES FIRST BASE safely and then overruns or overslides may immediately return without liability of being put out provided he does not attempt or feint an advance to second. A player who is awarded first base does not have this right.

ART. 5 . . . A RUNNER ACQUIRES THE RIGHT to the proper unoccupied base if he touches it before he is out. He is then entitled to this base until he is put out or until he legally touches the next base while it is unoccupied or until a following runner is forced (2-12-4) to advance to the base he has occupied.

PLAY (1)—While fielders try to tag out R^1 between second and third, R^2 advances to second. R^1 escapes to second. If one or both are on the base when tagged, which can be put out? RULING: If both are on the base only R^2, when tagged, is out. If only one is on the base when tagged, he is not out.

PLAY (2)—With R^1 on first, B^2 hits ground ball to F^3 who: (a) steps on first and then tags R^1 who has remained on first; or (b) tags R^1 while R^1 is on first and then steps on first. RULING: In (a), R^1 is not out since the force was removed when B^2 was put out. In (b), both R^1 and B^2 are out.

ART. 6 . . . EACH RUNNER SHALL TOUCH HIS BASE after the ball becomes dead unless he is awarded a base. The runner returns to the base he has reached or passed when the ball became dead except as follows. He returns to the base he occupied at the time **of the pitch** if his advance was: (a) during an uncaught foul; or (b) during a live ball period when a teammate or spectator or umpire interferes with a batted ball or when there is interference with an infielder or his throw when such throw was the first after fielding a batted ball and before it had been held by the pitcher in pitching position. In (b), if the runner's interference does not cause batter to be out and any other runner cannot return to the base he occupied at the time of the pitch, he is awarded the next base.

PLAY—What is the penalty for failing to retouch a base after ball becomes dead? RULING: No penalty is provided. Umpire should not order "Play ball" until runner is on or near such base.

Section 3.—Runner Awarded a Base

ART. 1 . . . EACH RUNNER other than the batter-runner (who is governed by 8-1-2) is awarded one base when:

a. There is a **balk** which is not ignored as in 6-2-5 Penalty; or a pitch strikes a runner; or

b. **He is forced** from the base he occupies by a following runner who must advance because a batter: receives a fourth ball; or is hit by a pitched ball; or hits a fair ball which becomes dead as in e or f of 5-1-1 or a or c of 5-1-2 or 5-1-3; or

c. **The catcher or any fielder interferes** with a batter (such as stepping on or across home base or pushing the batter to reach the pitch or touching the bat). See 8-1-1-e for ignoring the infraction and for batter also being awarded first base.

ART. 2 . . . WHEN A RUNNER IS OB-STRUCTED, while advancing or returning to a base, by a fielder who neither has the ball nor is attempting to field a batted ball, or while advancing only, a fielder without the ball fakes a tag, the umpire shall award the obstructed runner and each other runner affected by the obstruction the bases they would have, in his opinion, reached had there been no obstruction. The obstructed runner is awarded a minimum of one base beyond his position on base when the obstruction occurred. If any preceding runner is forced to advance by the awarding of a base or bases to an obstructed runner, the umpire shall award this preceding runner the necessary base or bases.

NOTE: When obstruction occurs the umpire gives the delayed dead ball signal and calls out "obstruction." If an award is to be made, the ball becomes dead when time is taken to make the award.

PLAY—With R^1 on second and R^2 on first, F^5, who neither has the ball nor is attempting to field a batted ball, obstructs R^1 when he is: (a) attempting to advance on a hit; or (b) returning to third after being trapped between third and home. RULING: In (a), R^1 and R^2 are awarded bases which they probably would have reached except for the obstruction. Until the ball is declared dead, R^2 may advance at his own risk. In (b), R^1 is awarded home base.

ART. 3 . . . EACH RUNNER is awarded:

a. **Four bases** (home) if a fair ball goes over a fence on fair ground in flight or is prevented from going over by being touched by a spectator or is touched by detached player equipment which is thrown, tossed, kicked or held by a fielder; or

b. **Three bases** if a batted ball (other than in item a) is touched by detached player equipment which is thrown, tossed, kicked, or held by a fielder provided the ball, when touched, is on or over fair ground, or is a fair ball while on or over foul ground, or is over foul ground in a situation such that it might become a fair ball; or

c. **Two bases** if a fair ball becomes dead because of touching a spectator other than as in item a or bounces over or passes through a fence; or if a live thrown ball: (1), including a pitch, is touched by detached player equipment which is thrown, tossed, kicked or held by a fielder; or (2) goes into a stand for spectators, or a player's bench, or over or through or lodges in a fence or touches a spectator and provided it is not by a pitcher from his plate as in item d; or

d. **One base** if a pitch or any throw by the pitcher from his pitching position on his plate goes into a stand or bench or over or through or lodges in a fence or backstop or touches a spectator or lodges in an umpire's equipment, or with less than two out the batter hits a fair or foul ball (fly or line drive) which is caught by a fielder, who then leaves the field of play by stepping with both feet or by falling into a bench, dugout, stand, bleacher; or over any boundary or barrier such as a fence, rope, chalk line, or pregame determined imaginary boundary line.

Illegal use of detached player equipment as in items a, b, or c does not cause ball to immediately become dead. If each runner advances to or beyond the base which he would reach as a result of the award, the infraction is ignored.

ART. 4 . . . AN AWARD IS FROM the base determined as follows: (1) If the award is the penalty for an infraction such as a balk without pitch being made or use of detached player equipment, measurement is from the base occupied at time of the infraction. If the infraction is a balk which is followed by a pitch, then the measurement is from base occupied at time of the pitch. (2) For an award, which does not involve any infraction as in (1), if any pitch (batted or unbatted) is followed by a dead ball before the pitcher is in position for the next pitch and before there is any throw by the fielding team, any award is from the base occupied at the time of the pitch. When a runner, who is returning to touch a base after a batted ball has been caught, is prevented from doing so because a thrown live ball has become dead, as in 5-1-1-f, his award shall be from the base he occupied at the time of the pitch. (3) In any situation other than (1) or (2), any award is from the base occupied when the ball last left the hand of the thrower. This would include any throw to a base by a pitcher while he is touching the pitcher's plate or any throw by any fielder following a batted or unbatted pitch.

PLAY—With R^1 on first, B^2 hits safely to

F^5 or to outfielder F^8. The throw is over or through F^3. RULING: If the overthrow does not become dead, there are no awards. If the overthrow becomes dead, two bases are awarded each runner (including the batter-runner) from the base he occupied when the throw left the hand of F^5 and F^8.

Section 4.—Runner Is Out

ART. 1 . . . THE BATTER-RUNNER is out when:

a. **He interferes** with the catcher's attempt to field the ball after a third strike; or

PLAY—B^1 has two strikes when he hits foul. Ball strikes catcher's mitt and rolls. As F^2 follows, B^1 moves into his path. RULING: Dead ball, hence no interference.

b. **His fair hit or his foul** (other than a foul tip which is not a third strike) is caught by a fielder; or such catch is prevented by a spectator reaching into the field enclosure; or his fair fly or fair line drive is intentionally dropped when a runner is on first and two are not yet out; or

NOTE: When a fair fly or fair line drive is dropped, any runner may advance at his own risk without retouching his base.

PLAY—R^1 is on first. One is out. B^3 hits fly ball to center field. (a) F^8 intentionally drops ball in an attempt to put out both R^1 and B^3; or (b) he juggles the fly ball but F^8 or F^7 catches the juggled ball before it touches the ground. RULING: (a) Umpire declares B^3 out and R^1 is not forced to leave first base. R^1 may advance at his own risk and without retouching first base. Unlike the infield fly rule, this rule covering intentional dropping of the ball (8-4-1-b) applies when at least first base is occupied and there are less than two out. (b) Legal catch. B³ is out and R¹ must retouch first base after ball is touched by F⁸.

c. **His bat hits the ball a second time** and the act is intentional or the bat is carelessly dropped or thrown in such a way as to strike the ball and deflect its course. This is interference and the ball becomes dead (5-1-2-b). If it is clearly accidental and the ball rolls into the bat, it is not interference; or

PLAY—B³ bunts. Ball in flight or on the ground in front of home base is hit as the batter's swing is completed or when he drops his bat. RULING: B³ is out. Ball becomes dead and each runner must return to his base.

d. **A third strike** is caught (usually by the catcher but might be by a fielder if ball rebounds from the catcher); or third strike is not caught while a runner is on first and fewer than two are out; or

PLAY—B¹ has two strikes. On the next pitch: (a) he hits foul ball which strikes umpire who is positioned behind F²; or (b) he strikes and misses and ball strikes catcher or umpire. In either (a) or (b), ball rebounds into hands of catcher or pitcher. RULING: In (a), ball became dead and B¹ is not out. In (b), ball is alive. If it touched the umpire, it is no longer in flight and it is not a catch. If it touched only the catcher, it is a catch and B¹ is out.

e. **After a third strike** or a fair hit: the ball

held by any fielder touches him before he touches first base; or any fielder, while holding the ball securely in a hand, touches first base with any part of his person or the ball before batter-runner touches first base; or

f. **He runs outside** the three-foot lines (last half of the distance from home base to first base), while the ball is being fielded or thrown to first base. EXCEPTION: This infraction is ignored if it is to avoid a fielder who is attempting to field the batted ball or if the act does not interfere with a fielder or a throw; or

g. **Any runner or retired runner interferes** (2-5-3) in a way which obviously hinders a possible double play at first base.

h. **He deliberately removes his head protector** during playing action unless the ball becomes dead without being touched by a fielder or unless the head protector is removed after the ball becomes dead following its touching by a fielder. When a batter-runner is declared out for removing his head protector, he is called out immediately.

ART. 2 . . . ANY RUNNER is out when he:

a. **Runs more than three feet away** from a direct line between bases to avoid being tagged or to hinder a fielder while the runner is advancing or returning to a base. EXCEPTION: This is not an infraction if a fielder, attempting to field a batted ball, is in the runner's proper path and if the runner runs behind the fielder to avoid interfering with him; or

b. **Intentionally interferes** with a throw or a thrown ball; or he hinders a fielder who is attempting to field a batted ball; or his being put out is prevented by an illegal act by anyone connected with the team as in 2-5-3, 3-2-2 and 3 or by the batter-runner. See 8-2-6 for runner returning to base; and 8-4-2-f for runner being hit by a batted ball. If in the judgment of the umpire, a runner or a retired runner (including the batter-runner) interferes in any way and prevents a double play anywhere, two shall be declared out (the interferer and the other runner involved). If the batter-runner interferes, the umpire shall call him out and the runner who has advanced the nearest to home base; or

NOTE: If two fielders try to field a batted ball and the runner contacts one or both, the umpire shall decide which one is entitled to field the ball and that fielder only is entitled to protection. If a fielder drops a batted ball and contact with a runner occurs during a subsequent attempt to field the ball, the fielder has the greater responsibility for avoiding contact.

c. **Is touched by** a live ball securely held by a fielder or is touched by a fielder's glove or hand with the live ball held therein, while the runner is not touching his base. EXCEPTIONS: If a batter-runner safely touches first base and then overslides or overruns it, he may immediately return to first base without liability of being tagged out, provided he did not attempt to run to second. Also, if any base comes loose from its fastening when any runner contacts it, such runner cannot be tagged out because the base slides away from him; or

NOTE: Ball is not securely held if it is dropped or juggled after the runner is touched, unless the runner deliberately knocks the ball from the fielder's hand.

d. **Does not retouch** his base before a fielder tags him out or holds the ball while touching such base after any situation as in 8-2-1, 2 and 3. EXCEPTIONS. If he is not put out before the next pitch, the need for retouching the base is ignored. Also, it is not necessary for runner to retouch his base after a foul tip (2-8-2) or when a batter is declared out because his fair hit is intentionally dropped as in 8-4-1-b; or

PLAY—R^1 is on first when B^2 hits line drive which is touched by F^4 and bounds off his glove to F^8 who catches it. R^1 leaves first after F^4 touched the ball but before the catch. RULING: Legal advance by R^1. B^2 is out.

e. **Fails to reach the next base** before a fielder either tags him out or holds the ball while touching such base, after runner has been forced from the base he occupied because the batter became a runner (with ball in play) when other runners were on first base, or on first and second, or on first, second, and third. EXCEPTION: No runner may be forced out if a runner who follows him in the batting order is first put out (including a batter-runner who is out for an infield fly); or

PLAY: With R¹ on second and R² on first, B³ hits a fair ground ball. Ball is thrown: (a) to second and then to third; or (b) to third and then to second; or (c) to third and then to first. In all cases, throw arrives before runner but runner is not touched with ball. RULING: (a) R² is out but R¹ is not. (b) Both R¹ and R² are out. (c) Both R¹ and B³ are out.

f. **Is hit by a batted fair ball** which is on or over fair ground and before it has touched a fielder or passed a fielder other than the pitcher. Any runner also is out when a fair ball on or over fair ground contracts him after passing through (but not touched), or by an infielder other than the pitcher and the umpire is positive another infielder had a chance to make a play with the ball had it not come in contact with the runner. EXCEPTION: If runner is touching his base when he is hit by an infield fly, he is not out but batter is out by the infield fly rule. Ball becomes dead, even in the exception. See 8-2-6 for runner returning to base; and 8-4-1-g for two being called out; or

NOTE: If runner is hit by infield fly when he is not touching his base, both he and the batter are out.

g. **Attempts to advance to home base** when the batter interferes with a play at home base, provided two are not already out; or

NOTE: If two are out, the batter is out because of his interference and since he is

the third out, the runner cannot score. But if two are not out, the runner is out and the batter is not penalized.

h. **Passes an unobstructed preceding runner** before such runner is out; or

i. **Runs bases in reverse** to confuse opponents or to travestize the game; or

j. **Deliberately removes** his head protector as in 8-4-1-h.

k. Positions himself behind a base to get a running start; or

l. When he does not slide or attempt to get around a fielder who has the ball and is waiting to make the tag. (See 3-3-1.)

PLAY—R^1 is on second and R^2 on first when B^3 hits. R^1 advances to home base but fails to touch third. R^2 touches second, third, and home, after which: (a) R^1 realizes his misplay and returns to third before ball is held on third; or (b) R^1 is declared out when ball is held on third and appeal is made. RULING: (a) in (a) the umpire will order R^1 to the bench because any runner who misses a base while advancing may not return to touch it after a following runner has scored. (b) R^2 is not out and his run is counted unless R^1 was the third out.

INTERPRETATION
When a Batter Becomes a Runner

A batter becomes a runner and may attempt to score when one of the following occurs:

1. He hits a fair ball.
2. He is charged with a third strike, but

the catcher drops the ball. (This situation was explained in the last chapter.)

3. He draws a walk.

4. He gets hit with the pitch. (This is ignored if the batter swings at the pitch, if the umpire calls it a strike, or if the umpire rules that the batter did not make an effort to avoid getting hit.)

5. The catcher interferes with the batter.

Touching, Occupying, and Returning to a Base

A runner advancing around the bases in an attempt to score must touch first, second, third, and home plate in that order. When returning to a base, the runner must also retouch the bases in reverse order. If a runner happens to miss a base, he may go back and retouch it as long as another runner has not gone past that base already. When a fly ball is caught, whether it be fair or foul, each runner is required to retouch his current base before advancing.

When a batter-runner advances to first base after hitting the ball, he has the right to overrun it and return to it safely. However, he must return to first base immediately, without a feint or attempt to move on to second base. A runner is allowed to turn to his left on his way back to first base, facing second, as long as he doesn't make a break towards the second base. This privilege does not apply to a runner who is awarded first base.

A runner may take possession of an unoccupied base if he touches it before being put out. He is entitled to this base until he is put out, forced to advance, or legally advances to the next base.

Each runner must retouch his current base before advancing unless he is awarded a base. The umpire should wait until all runners go back and retouch their bases before he orders "time in."

Runner Awarded a Base

As the umpire, you should award a one-base advance to a runner when:

1. There is a balk which has not been ignored.

2. The runner is forced from his base because a subsequent batter walked or got his base by a pitch.

3. The catcher or any other fielder interferes with the batter.

If a runner is obstructed by a fielder, you should award the runner the number of bases you feel the runner would have made if the obstruction had not occurred. Recently, a ruling was passed enforcing an obstruction call on a fielder when the fielder fakes a tag on the runner when he doesn't have possession of the ball. This often occurs at second base. The runner from first base isn't sure whether he should slide into second or not, because he doesn't know whether the fielder has the ball. The fielder pretends to have the ball, often causing the runner to slide needlessly, thinking it will be a close play. This may cause unnecessary injury to the runner who decides to slide at the last second.

A runner is awarded one base if the pitcher makes an overthrow (throws the ball out of bounds) while standing on the pitcher's plate. The runner is also awarded one base when there are less than two outs and the fielder's momentum carries him out of bounds after catching a fly ball.

Remember, foul territory is still in bounds. The out-of-bounds territory is designated before the game starts.

If any of the following occur, a runner is awarded two bases:

1. A fair batted ball is touched by a spectator.

2. A fair ball bounces over, through, or under a fence.

3. A live thrown ball, not coming from the pitcher's plate, goes out of bounds.

4. A live thrown ball is touched by detached player equipment.

A three-base award is given a runner when a fair batted ball is touched by detached equipment belonging to a member of the defensive team. This rule usually applies in the outfield when a fielder throws his glove in an attempt to stop a ball from rolling past him.

Finally, an umpire should award four bases to a batter if, for some reason, the batted fair ball is prevented from going over the outfield fence by anything other than a legal catch. This may happen if thrown player equipment obstructs the ball's trajectory or a spectator touches the ball. Of course, if the ball does clear the fence, it is considered a home run and a four-base advance is awarded. In both cases the umpire gives a delayed dead ball signal. If each runner advances up to or beyond the base awarded by the umpire, the call is ignored. If the call is ignored, the umpire should let the offending team know that such a call would have been made and also issue a warning to avoid future infractions.

When an award is given for detached player equipment, the runners are awarded their advances starting from the bases they occupied before the pitch. In any other situation, the advance is made from the base the runner occupied when the ball left the hand of the fielder.

Situation: Northern Arizona University is playing at Montana State University in a Big Sky Conference game. In the top of the fourth inning, the Northern Arizona lead-off batter draws a walk. The next batter bloops a short fly ball into right field, and neither the second baseman nor the right fielder are able to catch it. The runner on first base tags second and is on his way to third. The batter easily makes it to first base and begins taking a turn toward second. The right fielder retrieves the ball and tries to make a play on the runner going to third base. However, he hurries his throw, and the ball sails over the third baseman's head and goes out of bounds.

Ruling: This play calls for a two-base award, since the batter was between first and second base, and the other runner was between second and third when the ball left the outfielder's hand. The umpire correctly awards third base and home plate to the respective runners.

Umpires should note that sometimes coaches don't understand the rules and incorrectly request a "one-plus-one" ruling. They are asking by this request that a runner get the base he is going to, plus one more. In the example, a runner was going to third when the overthrow occurred. The coach wants him to get the base he is going to—third—plus one more—home. The runner is awarded home plate in this particular case, but only because it happens to be a two-base award. There is no such thing as "one-plus-one." All overthrows and awards are either one-, two-, three-, or four-base advancements.

Runner Is Out

The *batter-runner* is out when:

1. He interferes with the catcher after a dropped third strike.

2. His fair or foul fly ball is caught by a fielder. An umpire also may call the batter out if he believes that the fielder intentionally dropped the ball with men on first and second, or if a spectator prevents a fielder from catching a ball.

3. His bat intentionally hits the ball a second time. If the batter drops his bat after hitting the ball and it accidentally hits the fair ball that is rolling into the infield, no call is made. If the batter tries to knock the ball away from a fielder intentionally, the umpire should call him out.

4. A third strike is caught. If a third strike

is not caught, the batter is still out if a runner occupies first base and there are less than two outs.

5. After a dropped third strike or a fair hit, the ball is held by a fielder who touches first base before the batter can get there.

6. He runs outside the three-foot restraining lines that are located the last half of the distance between home and first base. This is common on a dropped third strike. The batter runs toward first base directly on the foul line and not inside the three-foot restraining lines as he should be. This causes the catcher to throw the ball over the runner in an attempt to reach the first baseman. More often than not, the ball sails into right field. This is not considered an overthrow. It should be ruled as interference. The umpire should declare a dead ball and call the batter out.

7. He interferes with a fielder in a way that prevents a possible double play at first base.

8. He deliberately removes his head protector during a live play.

A *runner* is out when any of the following occurs:

1. He runs outside the base paths, which include three feet on either side of the direct line from one base to another. This rule is ignored if the runner does this in order to avoid running into a fielder who is fielding a batted ball.

2. He intentionally interferes with a throw or hinders a fielder who is making a play on the ball.

3. He is tagged while not on a base with a live ball that is either in the gloved or bare hand of a fielder. This rule is ignored when the runner correctly overruns first base or when a base becomes unfastened after a player slides into it.

4. He doesn't retouch his base ("tag up") before advancing to the next base after a fielder catches a fly ball. In order to get this runner out, the defensive team tags the base the runner left.

5. He is forced to a base but before he is able to reach it he is either tagged out or is forced out by a fielder touching that base while holding the ball.

6. He gets hit by a batted ball before it has been touched by a fielder. If he is standing on a base and gets hit during an infield fly rule, he is not ruled out. The batter, however, is still out.

7. He tries to advance home while the batter is interfering with a play at home plate. This is only true when there are less than two outs. With two outs, the interfering batter is declared out, not the runner.

8. He passes a runner on the base paths who has not been put out.

9. He runs the bases in the wrong direction.

10. He deliberately removes his head protector while running.

11. He moves behind a base to get a running start toward the next one.

12. A runner tries to ram into a fielder to jar the ball away from him. He must slide legally or avoid a fielder who is chasing him.

10

Scoring and Record Keeping

RULE 9

Section 1.—How a Team Scores

ART. 1 . . . A RUNNER SCORES one run each time he legally advances to and touches first, second, third and then home base before three are out to end the inning. EXCEPTIONS: A run is not scored if the runner advances to home base during action in which the third out is made as follows: (a) by the batter-runner before he touches first base; or (b) by another runner being forced out; or (c) by the preceding runner who is declared out because he failed to touch one of the bases; or (d) when a third out is declared during a play in which an appeal is subsequently upheld on another runner, the appeal play decision takes precedence or; (e) when there is more than one appeal during any play which terminates a half-inning, the defensive team may select the out which is to its advantage.

NOTE: If a fielder illegally obstructs a runner and is responsible for failure of that runner to reach home base, umpire has authority to award home base to such runner.

PLAY (1)—R^1 is on second and R^2 on first when batter hits a home run inside the field. R^2 fails to touch second and appeal is made. The hit occurred: (a) when only one was out; or (b) when two were out. RULING: (a) R^2 is out. Both other runs score. (b) No run scores since R^2 is the third out by a force play.

PLAY (2)—With R^1, R^2 and R^3 on base and two out, B^6 hits a slow ground ball to F^6, who throws to second to put out R^3. R^1 touched home base before the out. RULING: No run is scored.

PLAY (3)—With two out, R^1 is on third and R^2 on second. B^5 hits. R^1 goes home and R^2 is tagged out near third. RULING: Not a force play, hence R^1 scores if he touched home base before the third out. Otherwise the run does not score.

PLAY (4)—With two out, R^1 is on third and R^2 on first. B^5 hits. R^1 reaches home. After this, R^2 is tagged out when he overslides second after touching it. RULING: Run by R^1 scores. The force ended when R^2 touched second.

PLAY (5)—With one out, R^1 is on third and R^2 on first. B^4 hits fly which is caught. R^1 tags up and goes home. After R^1 has touched home base, ball is thrown to first where R^2 has failed to tag up after the catch. RULING: The run by R^1 scores. Throwing the ball to first and appealing to umpire constitutes an appeal but it is not a force-out.

PLAY (6)—R^1, R^2 and R^3 are on third, second and first, respectively, with one out when B^5 hits fly ball to F^9 for second out. All three runners advance as ball is caught, however R^1 does not touch up. R^3 is tagged out by F^4 after R^1 has touched home base. The ball is then thrown to F^5 who appeals the infraction of R^1 at third. RULING: R^1 is out and his run is cancelled.

ART. 2 . . . THE NUMBER OF RUNS scored by each team is entered on the score card for each inning. The team whose runners score the greatest total number of runs for the entire regulation game (Rule 4-2) wins.

Section 2.—Recording Game Activity

ART. 1 . . . UNIFORMITY IN RECORDS of game activity is promoted by use of a standard tabulation sheet containing columns as shown in the diagram.

ART. 2 . . . THE OFFICIAL SCORER (as designated by the umpire in chief) shall keep records as outlined in the following rules. He has the final authority when judgment is involved in determining whether a batter-runner's advance to first base is the result of an error or of a base hit, and in similar situations.

Section 3.—Player's Batting Record

ART. 1 . . . EACH PLAYER'S batting record shall include:

a. In columns 1, 2 and 3 (after name and position), the number of times he batted

(See 2-18-2), the runs he scored (9-1-1), and the base hits he made (Art. 2); and

b. **In the summary,** the number of: total base hits and the type (single, double, triple or home run); sacrifice hits; and number of runs he batted in.

ART. 2 . . . A BASE HIT IS CREDITED to a batter when he advances to first base safely:

a. **Because of his fair hit** (rather than because of a fielder's error) EXCEPTION: It is not a base hit if any runner is out on a force play caused by the batter advancing toward first base; or

   NOTE: Base hits include any fair hit which cannot be fielded in time to throw out or tag out a batter-runner or any other runner when he is being forced to advance. Illustrations are: ball is stopped or checked by a fielder in motion who cannot recover in time; or ball moves too slowly; or ball is hit with such force to a fielder that neither he nor an assisting fielder can handle it.

b. **Without liability** of being put out because: a runner is declared out for being hit by the batted ball (8-4-2-f); or the umpire is hit by a batted ball as in 8-2-1-b; or

c. Because of a **fielder's choice** (2-8-3-Note) when a fielder attempts to put out another runner but is unsuccessful and the scorer believes the batter-runner would have reached first base even with perfect fielding.

ART. 3 . . . A BASE HIT FOR EXTRA BASES is credited to the batter when it is the sole reason for his safe arrival at second

OFFICIAL SCORE

BOX SCORE

Visiting Club
Players

10 center field	
3 right field	
7 third base	
9 left field	
8 catcher	
5 first base	
6 second base	
1 shortstop	
4 pitcher	

	1	2	3	4	5	6	7	8	9	10

	AB	R	H	PO	A	E

1 2 3 4 5 6

Earned Runs   Two-Base Hits   Three-Base Hits   Home Runs
Passed Balls   Wild Pitches   Bases on Balls   Struck Out   Left on Bases
Bases on Hit by Pitched Balls
Double Plays   Time

(double), third (triple), or home base (home run). EXCEPTION: If he is put out while oversliding second or third, he is credited with having reached such base.

PLAY—B¹ hits and advances to second and third, but in touching third, he overslides and is tagged out. RULING: Credit B¹ with a triple.

ART. 4 ... A SACRIFICE HIT is credited to the batter when, with not more than one out, his bunt enables any runner to advance or his fly ball enables a runner to score but which, in either case, results in the batter-runner being put out before he reaches first or would have resulted in his being put out if hit had been fielded without error.

PLAY—R¹ is on first with one out. B³: (a) bunts; or (b) swings and hits ball. In each case, R¹ advances safely to second. B³ is out before reaching first. RULING: Sacrifice in (a) but not in (b).

ART. 5 ... A RUN BATTED IN is credited to the batter when a runner scores because of: a base hit (including the batter-runner's score on a home run); a sacrifice hit; any put-out; a forced advance such as for a base on balls or batter being hit; or an error, provided two are not yet out and that action is such that the runner on third would have scored even if there had been no error. EXCEPTION: It is not a run batted in if there is a double play from a force or one in which the batter is put out.

ART. 6 . . . WHEN A STRIKE-OUT involves more than one batter, it is charged to the one who received at least two strikes. If no batter received more than one strike, it is charged to the batter who received the third strike.

Section 4.—Player's Base Running Record

ART. 1 . . . A STOLEN BASE shall be credited in the summary to a runner each time he advances a base without the aid of a base hit, a put-out, or a fielding (including battery) error. EXCEPTIONS: No runner is credited with a steal if: (1) after reaching the base, the runner overslides and is put out; or (2) in an attempted double or triple steal, any runner is put out; or (3) opponents are in collusion as in a deliberate attempt to help establish a record.

Section 5.—Player's Fielding Record

ART. 1 . . . EACH PLAYER'S FIELDING RECORD shall include: the times he put out a batter or runner; the times he assisted a teammate in putting out a runner; and the number of errors he committed. These shall be recorded respectively in columns 4, 5, and 6.

ART. 2 . . . A PUT-OUT IS CREDITED to a fielder who catches a batted ball in flight or who tags out a runner, or who puts out a runner by holding the ball while touching a base to which a runner is forced to advance or return. Special cases are: (1) CATCHER is credited with the put-out when batter is out for illegally batting the ball, or for a third strike bunted foul, or for batter being hit by his own batted ball, or for batting out of turn, or for failing to wear a head protector. (2)

For an INFIELD FLY, the put-out is credited to the fielder who would ordinarily have made the catch. (3) For runner being out because of BEING HIT by a batted ball, or for deliberately removing his head protector, the put-out is credited to the fielder who is nearest the ball at the time.

ART. 3 . . . AN ASSIST is credited to a fielder each time he handles or deflects the ball during action which is connected with the put-out or he handles the ball prior to an error which prevents what would have been a put-out. If several fielders handle the ball or one fielder handles it more than once during a play (such as when a runner is caught between bases), only one assist is credited to each of such fielders.

NOTE: After a pitch, if catcher tags out or throws out a runner, the pitcher is not credited with an assist.

ART. 4 . . . A DOUBLE PLAY OR TRIPLE PLAY is credited to one or more fielders when two or three players are put out between the time a pitch is delivered and the time the ball next becomes dead or is next in possession of the pitcher in pitching position.

ART. 5 . . . AN ERROR is charged against a fielder for each misplay which prolongs the time at bat of the batter; or the time a player continues to be a runner; or permits the runner to advance one or more bases. EXCEPTIONS: (1) **A pitcher** is not charged with an error for: a base on balls; or a batter being hit; or a balk; or a passed ball or wild pitch unless the batter advances to first base on such pitch (third strike).

(2) **A catcher** is not charged with an error for a wild throw in his attempt to prevent a stolen base unless the base stealer advances another base because of the wild throw.

(3) **Neither catcher nor infielder** is charged with an error for a wide throw in an attempt to complete a double play, unless the throw is so wild that it permits a runner to advance an additional base. But if a player drops a thrown ball when, by holding it, he would have completed the double (or triple) play, it is an error.

(4) **A fielder** is not charged with an error for accurately throwing to a base whose **baseman fails to stop** or try to stop the ball, provided there was good reason for such throw. If the runner advances because of the throw, the error is charged to the baseman, or fielder who should have covered that base.

(5) If a fielder **drops a fair fly ball** but recovers in time to force out a runner, he is not charged with an error. It is recorded as a force-out.

PLAY (1)—On third strike on B^1, catcher F^2 drops the ball or ball goes past him. B^1 advances to first. RULING: Error charged to catcher. It is not a "passed ball." Pitcher is credited with strikeout.

PLAY (2)—B^1 bats fair hit. Ball is thrown to F^3 on first in time to put out B^1 but F^3 fails to touch base and B^1 is safe. RULING: Error charged to F^3. The same ruling applies to any force play.

Section 6.—Pitcher's Record

ART. 1 . . . A WILD PITCH shall be charged

in the summary to the pitcher when a ball legally delivered to the batter is so high, or so low (including any pitch which touches the ground in front of home base), or so far away from home base that the catcher does not stop or control it with ordinary effort so that the batter-runner advances to first base or any runner advances a base.

NOTE: When the catcher enables a runner (other than the batter-runner) to advance by failing to control a pitch, which he should have been able to control, it is not a wild pitch but a "passed ball." For dropping third strike see Play 1 under Sec. 5.

ART. 2 . . . THE NUMBER OF: bases on balls; batters being hit by a pitch; strike-outs; and base hits allowed by each pitcher shall be recorded in the summary. If batter is hit by what would have been the fourth ball, it is recorded as a hit batter.

ART. 3 . . . In order for a run to be earned, it must be scored without the aid of errors or passed balls. To determine whether runs are earned or not, reconstruct the inning without the errors and passed balls. If there is doubt as to whether or not a run is earned, the pitcher shall be given the benefit.

PLAY—Is a run earned when it results from: catcher interference which sends batter to first and forces runner home; or a passed ball; or a fielder's error; or failure of fielding team to make reasonable effort to retire the opponent? RULING: No.

ART. 4 . . . A STRIKE-OUT is credited to the pitcher when a third strike is delivered to a batter even though the batter might reach first base because the third strike is a wild pitch or is not caught. It is also a strikeout if an attempted third strike bunt is an uncaught foul.

ART. 5 . . . A RELIEF PITCHER shall not be charged with any earned run scored by a runner who was on base when such pitcher entered nor with any hit or advance by a batter who had more balls than strikes when such pitcher entered.

ART. 6 . . . WINNING AND LOSING PITCHERS are determined as follows:

1. If the starting pitcher has pitched the first four innings or more and his team is ahead when he is replaced and it holds the lead for the remainder of the game he shall be the winning pitcher.

2. If the starting pitcher cannot be declared the winning pitcher under the provisions in item 1 above, and more than one relief pitcher plays, the winning pitcher shall be determined under the following criteria:

a. If the score is tied it results in the game becoming a new contest so far as judging who is the winning and losing pitcher.

b. If the starting pitcher is lifted before having pitched four or more innings and his team is ahead, the official scorer shall determine the winning pitcher to be the relief pitcher who has been the most effective.

c. When the opposition goes ahead, pitchers up to that time in the game cannot be credited with the win other than the pitcher against whose pitching when the opponents took the lead, remains in the game, and his team subsequently goes ahead and maintains its lead the rest of the game.

d. Generally the relief pitcher credited with the win is the pitcher when his team takes the lead and holds it for the rest of the game. However, if the relief pitcher pitches only a short while or not effectively and a succeeding relief pitcher replaces him and does better work in keeping the lead the latter shall be granted the win.

3. If a pitcher is lifted for a pinch hitter or a pinch runner, the runs scored by his team during the inning of his removal are to be credited to his benefit to decide the pitcher of record when his team takes the lead.

4. The starting pitcher shall be charged with the loss when he is replaced and his team is behind or falls behind because of runs assessed to him after being replaced and his team does not subsequently tie the score nor take the lead.

5. A pitcher cannot be given credit for pitching a shutout when he does not pitch the complete game except when he enters the game with no one out before the opponents have scored in the first inning and does not permit the opposition to score during the game.

ART. 7 . . . SAVES by relief pitchers are determined as follows:

1. A relief pitcher who enters the game and holds his team's lead for the remainder of the game shall be credited with a save unless he is credited with the win.

2. A relief pitcher who does not finish the game cannot be credited with a save except when he is taken out because of a pinch-hitter or pinch-runner.

3. Only one save can be granted for a game. When two or more relief pitchers meet the specifications of this rule, the official scorer shall give the save to the pitcher he judges to have done the best job in effectiveness.

Section 7.—General Summary

ART. 1 . . . THE GAME SUMMARY includes the following:

1. Total score and runs scored in each inning.

2. Stolen bases for each runner.

3. Sacrifice hits by each batter.

4. Base hits by each batter and total against each pitcher.

5. Two- or three-base hits, and home runs.

6. Times at bat for each player and total against each player.

7. Strike-outs by each pitcher.

8. Bases on balls by each pitcher.

9. Wild pitches by each pitcher.

10. Times each pitcher hits batter with pitch—also names of those hit.

11. Passed balls by catcher.

12. Time required to play game and name of each umpire.

ART. 2 . . . PERCENTAGE RECORDS are computed as follows:

1. Percentage of games won and lost, divide the number of games won by the total games won and lost.

2. Batting average, divide the total number of base hits (not the total bases on hits), by the total times at bat.

3. Fielding average, divide the total put-outs and assists, by the total of put-outs, assists, and errors.

4. Pitcher's percentage, divide the total runs earned during his pitching by the total number of innings he pitched (average runs per inning); and multiply by 7 (average runs per game).

NOTE: In items 1, 2, 3 or 4, if there is a fraction of ½ or more, a full point is added.

INTERPRETATION

A team scores a run each time a runner legally advances around the bases to home plate before the team has accumulated three outs. There are exceptions to this rule. A scoring run does not count when the batter is out before he touches first base or if another runner is forced out. A run also does not count in some situations when an appeal is made during a play that determines the third out.

The team scoring the most runs by the end of the game is declared the winner.

Recording Game Activity

The official scorer is responsible for keeping accurate records of the game. He records the following:

1. The final score, as well as the score by innings.

2. Stolen bases.

3. Sacrifice hits.

4. Hits made by each batter and total hits against each pitcher.

5. Individual times at bat for each batter and total number of batters that each pitcher faces.

6. Strike-outs.

7. Walks.

8. Wild pitches.

9. The number of times a pitcher hits a batter. (The names of the hit players must also be included.)

10. Passed balls.

11. Time required to play the game.

12. Names of every umpire

These records are kept on a standard tabulation sheet. The entries also are recorded in the game summary. The scorer records action throughout the game to accumulate the totals for the game summary.

Batting Record

During the game, the scorer records the number of times each player bats, the number of runs he scores, and the base hits that he makes. At the end of the game, the scorer records both the batter's total number and type of base hits (single, double, and so on) as well as his total runs batted in.

The scorer credits a batter for a hit when he advances to first base safely after one of the following has occurred:

1. He gets a fair hit. It is not considered a hit—even when a batter makes it to first safely—if his batted ball causes a runner to

be put out on a forced play. Nor does it count as a hit if a fielder commits an error.

2. If a runner or umpire is hit by a batted ball, the ball is automatically dead. However, if the scorer believes that the ball would have been a completed hit if it had remained alive, he may credit the batter with a hit.

3. If the scorer believes the batter would have made it to first safely during an unsuccessful fielder's choice even if the fielder tried to put out the batter right away, without the interceding play, the scorer may credit the batter with a hit.

If a batter hits safely and advances to second, third, or home only because of that hit, he is credited with, respectively, a double, triple, or home run. If the batter-runner happens to overslide second or third and in the process is tagged out, he is still credited with having reached that base.

A sacrifice hit may occur when there are less than two outs. Sacrifice hits enable a base-runner to score from third on a fly ball. They also may allow a base runner to advance one base on a successful bunt by the batter. In either case, the runner is put out at first base. A sacrifice does not count in the scorebook as an official time at bat.

A batter is credited with a run batted in (RBI) when a runner scores on a base hit, a sacrifice hit, or an error (with less than two outs, providing the run would have scored if no errors had occurred).

In situations where a strike-out involves more than one batter, the strike-out is charged to the batter who received at least two of the strikes.

Base Running Record

If a base runner advances on his own without the aid of a base hit, put out, walk, error, wild pitch, or passed ball, he is credited with a stolen base. If, however, the runner is tagged out after oversliding a base, or if during a double or triple steal any of the runners are put out, no stolen base is recorded or credited to any of the runners.

Fielding Record

The scorer records the number of put outs and assists each player makes, along with the number of errors he commits.

A fielder is credited with a put out when he catches a batted ball in flight, tags out a runner, or touches a base while holding the ball when a runner is forced to that base.

The catcher gets credit for a put out when the batter: illegally hits the ball, bunts the ball foul on a third strike, is hit by his own batted ball, or fails to wear a head protector. (Umpires should not have to make such a call, because players shouldn't be allowed to bat without a helmet in the first place.)

When a runner gets hit by a batted ball or deliberately removes his head protector while running, the fielder nearest to the ball is credited with the put out.

An assist occurs when a player touches the ball during the action connected with the put out. One assist per player is the maximum awarded for any one play. If a catcher tags or throws a runner out after a pitch, the pitcher does not get credited with an assist.

A double or triple play occurs when two or three players are put out during one continuous action. These put outs are credited to the fielders responsible for getting the players out.

An error occurs when a fielder's misplay: prolongs the batter's time at bat, prolongs the time a player is a runner, or allows a runner to advance on the bases. There are a number of exceptions to the last part of this rule. They include the following:

1. A pitcher is not charged with an error for a walk, hit batsman, or balk. Also, a pitcher is not charged with a wild-pitch error unless the batter is able to make it to first, or the batter-runner is able to reach first base on a dropped third strike.

2. A catcher is not charged with an error for a wild throw if he is trying to prevent a stolen base and the runner does not advance past that base. An error is not charged to the catcher on a passed ball unless it allows a runner to make it to first base (as on a dropped third strike).

3. No player is charged with an error for a wild throw attempting to get the second out in a double play, unless the throw was so wild that it enabled the runner to advance one additional base. If a player drops a thrown ball and he would have completed a double play if he had held onto it, he is charged with an error.

4. A fielder is not charged with an error if his accurate throw is not caught by a team-

mate. The player who misses the ball is charged with an error only if the runner is able to advance.

5. If a fielder drops a ball but recovers it in time to get a runner or batter-runner out, he is not charged with an error.

In conclusion, note that there are two different types of errors: throwing errors and fielding errors.

Pitcher's Record

The scorer charges a wild pitch to the pitcher when he pitches the ball to the batter so high, so low, or so far from the plate that the catcher cannot catch it with ordinary effort and a runner or batter-runner advances.

All walks, strike-outs, hit batsmen, and base hits are also recorded for the pitcher's record in the game summary.

A pitcher's earned run average is very important. Errors and passed balls are not used to calculate this figure; only runs that are "earned" by the pitcher are counted toward the average. A relief pitcher is not charged with earned runs scored by a runner who was already on base when that pitcher entered the game.

A pitcher is credited with a strike-out when he gets a third strike on a batter, even if the batter is able to advance to first base. He also is credited with a strike-out if an attempted bunt is a foul ball on a third strike.

The scorer must look at several factors to determine the winning and losing pitchers. The scorer considers the following:

1. If the starting pitcher lasts four innings or more and his team has the lead when he is replaced, he is the winning pitcher if his team is able to hold that lead.

2. If the starting pitcher is removed before he pitches four innings and his team is ahead, the scorer chooses the most effective relief pitcher as the winning pitcher.

3. Usually, a relief pitcher comes into the game when his team is losing. If his team then takes and holds the lead, he is declared the winning pitcher.

4. If a pitcher is replaced by a pinch-hitter or pinch-runner, the runs scored by his team during that inning count on his behalf when the scorer determines the winning and losing pitchers.

5. The starting pitcher is charged with a loss if he is replaced while his team is losing and they fail to catch up and tie or take the lead.

A relief pitcher is credited with a save if he enters the game with the lead and holds it for the remainder of the game. A relief pitcher may finish the game to be credited with a save, with one exception: if the pitcher is replaced by a pinch-hitter or pinch-runner. The scorer may only grant one save per game, although sometimes more than one pitcher meets the requirements. When this happens, the scorer determines which pitcher was most effective.

To be an efficient scorer, you must calculate accurate percentages. Below are the formulas used to determine the percentages:

Percentage of games won and lost

$$\frac{\text{Total number of games won}}{\text{Total number of games played}}$$

Example: 10 games won, 5 lost

$$\frac{10}{15} = .666$$

Batting average

$$\frac{\text{Total number of hits}}{\text{Total number times at bat}}$$

Example: 25 hits, 75 at bats

$$\frac{25}{75} = .333$$

Fielding average

$$\frac{\text{Total number put outs and assists}}{\text{Total chances (put outs, assists, errors)}}$$

Example: 36 put outs and assists, 40 total chances

$$\frac{36}{40} = .900$$

Pitcher's earned run

$$\frac{\text{Total runs earned}}{\text{Total number of innings pitched}} \times 7$$

Example: 6 earned runs, 21 total innings

$$\frac{6}{21} \times 7 = 2.00$$

Situation

In a National Junior College Tournament played in St. Louis, a Houston, Texas, team is playing the state champion team from Maryland in the championship game. The Maryland team has a unique record—their pitchers have not allowed one walk during the entire season! It is the top of the sixth inning, and a Texas player is at bat. The pitcher gets into a three-ball, no-strike count, and it looks certain that the Maryland record will be broken. The pitcher will not give up the batter, however, and quickly works the count back up to three and two. His sixth pitch is thrown off target. It would have been ball four, but it hits the batter on the arm. The batter is awarded first base.

Ruling

The official scorer records that the batter was hit by a pitch, not walked. The scorer's entry is correct, leaving the Maryland record intact.

Index

U